BECOME THE ACE

13 Ways to Developing Peace, Passion, and Purpose

MICHAEL UNKS

Become the Ace:

13 Ways to Developing Peace, Passion, and Purpose

I'm providing you the audio version of this book FREE!

Click the link below

Click Here for the Audio Version

Also check out michaelunks.com for more free audio books!

Also check out my YouTube Channel

I can let you know when my next book comes out if you click the link below.

Keep me posted

Copyright © 2016 Michael Unks

Table of Contents

Become the Ace

Introduction

Do you ever think about what you're truly capable of? You are capable of becoming an **Ace** in life.

The **Ace** is a symbol of excellence. It can win all battles in life just like in the card game war.

It is the highest valued card in poker and black jack. In baseball, if a team needs a win, they send their ace to the mound.

You can make a difference in this world. You can offer something **no one** else can. You need to believe it or no one else will. Here's the problem…

You've heard this many times but you don't truly believe it.

Become the Ace

This book presents you with information at a different angle. It includes several embarrassing personal stories, like my first kiss where I was told, "You're a bad kisser. You need to work on that." It also includes references to several psychology terms and studies as well as references to popular tv shows such as *How I Met Your Mother*, *Breaking Bad*, *The Office*, and more.

The problem isn't not knowing. The problem is that it hasn't been presented in a way that sticks. It hasn't been presented in a way that causes long-lasting changes to your thinking and actions.

I made drastic changes in my life a couple years ago and it's because I started thinking about new ways to emotionally grasp what it takes to be successful. I started writing these things down and sharing them in hopes that others will get the same results. I know you can become an ace! If you haven't already, you just need to hear principles of success in a new way by reading the thirteen chapters in this book.

One thing you'll love about applying what's discussed in this book is that you'll be able to feel

Become the Ace

happy immediately! No matter where you currently are in life, you'll learn to operate in a state of mind of where you're going, not where you currently are. You'll feel like an ace on the inside while you start your journey of becoming an ace on the outside.

I carried an ace playing card in my wallet wherever I went, and whenever I was doubting myself and wanted to quit, I looked at the ace I had with me and it helped me to keep pursuing my dream. I applied these ideas discussed in this book so routinely that I realized I didn't need to carry the card with me anymore.

Instead, I gave the ace to someone that needed it more than me. I told him, "I see an Ace when I look at you," handed him the card and told him to look at it and remind himself that he'll do something great with his life.

Around this time I decided it was time to sharing the "Ace" idea with everyone. I bought several decks of cards and every time I handed out an ace the person's face would light up and I could see they were on their way to reaching their potential.

Become the Ace

I **promise** you'll read material on topics you may know, **but** it will be presented in ways you've never heard before. You may laugh at some of the things I've done, but it was a lesson for me and my hope is that it will be a lesson for you.

Inaction is the most common reason there aren't many Aces in life. This book is short. You can even read it in one sitting. What if just *one* idea in this book leads to taking a step in the right direction, the path to becoming the Ace I know you're meant to be? You have something incredible to offer this world, but it involves finding the motivation to put in the work. This book can offer you that.

Decide to become the Ace now! Decide to see yourself the way I already see you! Read this book and reach your potential and inspire everyone around you to reach their potential too. Plus, do this all with a smile on your face.

The world needs more Aces. Are you ready to become one?

Chapter 1

―◦―

Belief

"Belief creates the actual fact."

— William James

You will *not* become an ace in life if you don't believe it.

The idea of using an ace as a symbol of excellence came to me shortly after listening to Earl Nightingale's audio of the Strangest Secret. He

Become the Ace

opens by talking about one hundred men that are age twenty-five and explains how they're hopeful for the future.

He then mentions how well all these men did financially by the time they were 65. One was rich, four were financially independent, five were still working, thirty-six were dead, and the remaining were dependent on other people or agencies for money. He explained only five percent made were considered successful.

All of these men were on level playing fields, but what made the select few successful was their thoughts. As Buddha put it, "what we think, we become." There are many qualities needed to develop to become the best you can be, but it all starts with belief in yourself.

Everyone has heard that they are unique like a snowflake. You've also heard that you're special and to go do anything you want in life. However, only a select few *really* believe this. It may be because you compare yourself to others and allow yourself to be defined by everyone else.

Become the Ace

Beliefs are powerful. The following study done by psychologist Robert Rosenthal illustrates this. The experiment tested out the "observer-expectancy effect," which is that reality can be positively or negatively influenced by the expectations of others (1).

Students of a California elementary school were given an IQ test that was not discussed with the teachers. The teachers were told by those running the study that about twenty percent of students (selected at random by the testers) were "intellectual bloomers" and would be expected to do better than fellow classmates.

Later on in the school year, the students were tested again. All IQ scores went up, but there was a statistically significant gain in the "intellectual bloomers." It was believed that the teachers gave those perceived as gifted more attention and support. The teachers expected those select students to do well and made more of an effort to ensure they did.

This study highlights the "Pygmalion effect," which explains that higher expectations are proportional

Become the Ace

to increased performance. Some people are fortunate enough to have people in their lives to help them see themselves as "bloomers." It seems many successful people have had mentors in their lives who had a tremendous impact on them.

Notable mentors throughout history are: Mahatma Gandhi as a mentor to Martin Luther King Jr. and Nelson Mandela, Andrew Carnegie as a mentor to Charles Schwab, Benjamin Graham as a mentor to Warren Buffet, and Socrates as a mentor to Plato, who in turn was a mentor to Aristotle.

Mentors can bring out the best in you, but certain people and situations can bring out the worst in you. This is when the "golem effect" occurs. It explains that lower expectations lead to decreased performance.

Back to our deck of cards. We are not dealt the same card in life. Some people are dealt a "King" or a "Queen" in life while others are dealt a "2" or "3." If you take yourself at face value and feel you can't grow or change, you will likely fall victim to the "golem effect." You will have people come in your life who can be positive influences for you, those

Become the Ace

who see something in you that you can't see in yourself.

However, nothing will change until you decide to see it for yourself. The entire world can see something great when they look at you, but it will mean nothing if *you* don't see it. The fastest way to become successful is to see yourself as an Ace on the inside.

There is magic in believing. I found this out in pharmacy school. A big part of pharmacy school is learning about medications and looking at the trials that provide evidence to support their use. When a drug is scheduled for approval it gets compared with a placebo. The goal is to have the medication have a significant difference from the placebo.

Studies are designed so the patient doesn't know if he or she is getting the drug or a placebo. What shocked me is that the patients who took the placebo almost always had some sort of benefit. It didn't matter if the drug was for blood pressure, cholesterol, to quit smoking, to cure a form of cancer, or any other condition.

Become the Ace

There is magic in believing. Think about what people consider lucky - a rabbit's foot, picking up a penny that is head-side up, or finding a four-leaf clover. It's not the actual items that make you lucky, it's your *belief* in those items. When you believe you're lucky you focus on situations that validate that belief. Those situations might have been present all along, but it wasn't until that change in belief that you began to feel lucky.

Horoscopes are another example. Have you ever been shocked to find your prediction was accurate? A lot of times your prediction is vague and can apply to many people, but it's your self-fulfilling prophecy that often makes your description align.

A self-fulfilling prophecy is when a person unknowingly causes a prediction to come true, due to the simple fact that he or she expects it to come true. All that we've talked about in this chapter revolves around this idea. Most people are using it the wrong way.

For example, whenever I ask people how they're doing on a Monday it's almost always negative. The response I get isn't how they're feeling, it's often,

Become the Ace

"It's Monday," and they say it with a frown on their face. Because people think that Mondays are bad, they will unknowingly focus on all that's going wrong with the day and will often make every Monday a bad day.

Given the nature of my job, I've probably worked in fifteen different locations and I'm constantly meeting new people. When I work with someone new I like to tell them, "I have a feeling that today is going to be an awesome day," even on Mondays. I get strange looks, but I say this to use their self-fulfilling prophecies the way they should be used - to make you happy and more successful.

It brings a smile to my face at the end of the day when people tell me, "Today was awesome! I can't believe I'm saying this, because I normally hate my job." It's foolish to *expect* to have a bad day. It makes more sense to believe that your day is going to go well and look for reasons to validate that belief.

The best place to begin your journey of becoming an ace starts with thinking big. If you haven't read *The Magic of Thinking Big* by Dr. David J. Schwartz, I

Become the Ace

highly recommend it. It's a classic that has sold over six million copies. There is an excellent explanation of the concept of self-fulfilling prophecy in the beginning of the book.

It explains how one man was making five times as much as his colleagues with the same skill set simply because he believed big. Because he believed, his behavior and actions made him more successful.

It starts with belief. It's hard for me to see people settle in life, to not dream big. The main response I get is that they don't want to be disappointed when it doesn't work out. With this mindset you won't reach your potential. Expectations have been proven to be proportional to results through self-fulfilling prophecies.

It doesn't matter where you are in your life right now. It doesn't matter your age, level of education, or experience. Start to think about where you want to be in all areas of your life. Your physical appearance, where you are professionally, you name it.

Become the Ace

Don't hold back. The bigger you dream, the better. Thinking about who you want to become once will not make a difference. However, thinking about this often will. Also, writing down all the actions and behaviors you'll need to engage in to make what you want a reality is crucial.

We all have a strong need to stay consistent to how we see ourselves. Seeing yourself at your best will naturally pull you in the direction to make what you think a reality. There is one concern you may have. You may think you'll come accross full of yourself or possibly delusional.

The simple way to avoid this is to know where you are in the current moment and keep your aspirations to yourself. People may laugh at you anyway when you tell them your plans. That is because people look at you at face value, not who who you are on this Earth to become.

Here is a simple example of how believing in yourself helps you do what you thought was impossible. Let's say you want to become a physician, but you feel you aren't smart enough.

Become the Ace

Maybe people have told you that you can't do it, or you've made poor grades in school.

But you start to believe you *can* become a doctor. You visualize yourself wearing a stethoscope and saving people's lives. Whenever you have downtime- whether it's waiting in line, sitting in traffic, or showering - you picture yourself as a doctor. It puts a smile on your face and gives you hope. The more you think about your dream, the more you believe it can happen.

Now it's time for you to ask, "what will it take to make this happen?" Because you have such a strong need to stay consistent with how you see yourself, the answers start flowing at a rapid rate. You may write down: "study three hours a day, get a part-time job to hire a tutor, shadow doctors and ask for advice, research all the requirements for applying to medical school, buy a stethoscope and look at it whenever I'm losing motivation or starting to doubt myself, etc."

The wonderful thing about the pursuit of making your dream a reality is that you don't have to have all the answers right away. You *must* believe it can

Become the Ace

be possible, though. With belief just about anything you want to do in life is possible.

You're on this earth for a reason. You *are* special and you *do* have something amazing to offer this world. Please don't roll your eyes when someone tells you this. Believing this is true is the first step to doing something amazing and special with your life.

Don't just think about this once. This should be a daily practice. This is why many successful people spend time reading or listening to something positive and inspirational on a daily basis. If you constantly think about reaching your potential and experiencing happiness you will almost certainly get it.

It's possible you don't know exactly what you're meant to do in life, but believe you're here to do something big. Again, expectations are proportional to results. *Expect* to do something incredible with your life, and you may find that you'll become an ace no matter what card you started with.

You won't need a genie to grant you wishes anymore when you realize the power of thought. I

Become the Ace

hope you sincerely believe you have something to offer the world now. If you ever wonder how ordinary people do extraordinary things, it's because they have an "ace up their sleeve," and this represents the belief in themselves.

The next chapter will help you find out what exactly you want to do with your life by sparking your desire.

Chapter 2

Desire

"If you get a big enough why, you can always figure out how."

— Tony Robbins

One great way to spark desire is to find a way to increase the neurotransmitter dopamine, often described as the "motivation" molecule.

Become the Ace

The reward center in your brain releases dopamine when you do something pleasurable. Scientists believe dopamine was originally designed to make us repeat activities that would help the species survive, such as eating or mating. Over time we've evolved so that the brain can also release dopamine while we're doing other activities.

One of the healthiest ways to trigger dopamine is through succeeding while working towards a worthy ideal.

What does it mean to be successful? Everyone has their own definition. I love the one from Earl Nightingale: "Success is the progressive realization of a worthy ideal." Making your dream come true is often a worthy goal or ideal.

I was hoping to put a statistic here on the percentage of people who know what their dream is and how many of them are actively pursuing it. I didn't put it because a majority of people don't have a dream. It's because they're taught to be realistic from a young age. Most have a desire, but it's focused in the wrong area. The desire to be safe, the desire to be average, the desire to settle.

Become the Ace

Life isn't exciting when you don't have a purpose. Life is an amazing thing and you aren't here to simply exist. You are here to share your gifts and talents that are already within you and do something memorable with your life.

The memorable life involves desire. According to Napoleon Hill, author of "Think and Grow Rich," desire is the starting point of all achievement and the first step towards riches. Maybe you're thinking, "I already know this, but I don't have a strong desire for anything. I have no clue what I should do with my life." Ask yourself these questions. Don't just gloss over them. Actually take some time and think about it.

1. What breaks your heart?

I found it bizarre that I was in church and the pastor was talking about difference makers and how to find your calling right as I was writing this chapter. Your calling should involve improving the lives of others, and finding what's causing them pain and offering them relief is a way to find your calling.

What breaks my heart is seeing people who are depressed, have low self-esteem, and feel hopeless.

Become the Ace

What breaks my heart is people just existing in their life instead of making an exciting and fulfilling adventure.

I lived most of my life this way and I know how painful it is. I know helping these people is my calling in life. It's what drives me to put in eighty hour weeks and what drives me to keep taking action even when it's difficult or uncomfortable.

What breaks your heart? There is one thing I'm sure you feel strongly about. The answer may not come to you immediately because it's a tough question. Keep it in the back of your mind and I know you'll find the answer soon.

2. What would you do if you knew you couldn't fail?

Look at failure this way: if you look at success as coming closer to making your dream a reality, no matter how small, then the only way you'd be failing is if you aren't improving or you give up. I've changed the way I view failure. I used to think that dreams were for foolish people and you should find a job in demand that pays well. I also thought taking a year off from college to travel and "find

Become the Ace

yourself" was a waste of time. *These people needed to grow up and get a job*, I thought.

Why do I think differently now? Because you're not *supposed* to settle in life. You're not *supposed* to live a meaningless life that drains you. Growing up I never took the time to find my burning desire and find my purpose. I know many people in their twenties have a lot of anxiety because they feel they have no direction or purpose. Pursuing something exciting is a way to avoid failure.

Plus, living the "dream" is *more* about experiencing the positive emotions of joy, happiness and fulfillment in abundance and *less* about earning a specific salary or winning a particular award. Remember, *you* define your *own* success and working towards actualizing that success makes you successful.

3. If external rewards didn't exist, what career would you choose?

By "external rewards" I mean money, fame, praise, and all of the other material possessions we link with living the dream. For example, if you're a

Become the Ace

writer, could you publish your work under a pen name?

Would you still pursue your dream if someone else got all the credit for your success? If you can answer yes to this you truly love what you're doing and you have a great chance of having a fulfilling life.

Many of us look at celebrities as super human, when in actuality they just had a burning desire to be great, worked hard, and surrounded themselves with a team of people to help them succeed. I know your dreams can come true, but pursue them because you love it, not because you'll love the external rewards it will bring you.

Not focusing on the external can help you find your purpose. To quote the wise Earl Nightingale again, "Your returns in life must be in direct proportion to what you give." That means if you aren't getting paid externally you *must* receive satisfaction from another source.

This is why volunteering makes you feel good. You don't get paid, but you *must* be rewarded for what you give. Knowing you made someone's life better is a feeling worth a lot more than money. Getting

Become the Ace

thanked would be great, but be prepared to give without being appreciated. That way, if you get thanked, it will be a wonderful surprise.

Many people have a talent for something that doesn't pay well or is in a field in low demand. This prevents them from living their purpose. This prevents them from living their best life. Their dopamine levels drop because pursuing something just for external rewards doesn't make one successful. A desire to fulfill a worthy ideal does.

4. How do I know if what I enjoy is my calling?

This is something I thought of recently. I would ask people what they want to do with their lives and often they didn't know. I'd ask what they like doing and I heard "lifting weights," "watching TV and movies," and "playing video games."

I then told them if they ever thought of making it a career. After hearing several times that if they made a career out of it that it would no longer be fun I realized that telling people to pursue their hobbies may be poor advice. It's great to have an escape, as long as it's not destructive. For example, taking a break and scheduling an hour to watch your

Become the Ace

favorite show with a loved one is fine. However, mindlessly watching 40-plus hours of TV a week would be getting in the way of reaching your potential.

I've realized many people are afraid to make a career out of something because it will get repetitive and boring over time. This causes them to never live out their calling. I worked with a girl, Mary, who was struggling with this.

She was considering being a pharmacist, nurse, lawyer, and several other careers. I could tell right away Mary was determined enough to do just about anything.

"I can't pick anything because I need variety. I can't do something that's repetitive," she remarked. I replied, "I think what you want in a career may not be possible. No matter what you want to do in life, it's going to be repetitive. Focusing on what you do for other people makes it exciting."

Whenever I have down time I like to share personal stories, metaphors, and quotes to get people inspired. This night was no different. I told her, "I know for a fact my dream is to be a professional

Become the Ace

speaker and writer. Think about all the stories I've told you tonight. I've told them before, and it's possible I'll tell them thousands of times throughout my life. It's *very* repetitive.

But it's new to you, and I deliver it with the same enthusiasm the first time I told it to someone. Let's say you become a pharmacist; you're going to counsel people on the same medication thousands of times, but they haven't heard it and the knowledge you give them improves their health. It's repetitive, but it feels good every time making someone's life better."

She paused for a moment and said one of the phrases I now live for: "I never thought about it that way before." Has the fear of repetition held you back? You can't avoid it, but you can change how you feel about it by looking at another person's perspective.

You are truly fortunate if your calling lies in your career. However, sometimes your burning desire lies in what you do outside of your job. Whatever you do in life, you have to be living out a purpose that is memorable.

Become the Ace

What if you want to make a career from your calling? It's simple. You can't just like it, you have to *love* it. This is a perfect time to share a quote I collected after reading *The Entrepreneur Roller Coaster* by Darren Hardy: "Work is gonna suck 95% of the time. But that other 5% is freaking awesome!"

Maybe you thought after reading that quote, "That can't possibly be true. It has to be 'freaking awesome' more than 5% of the time."

Let's take professional athletcs as an example. Winning a championship is awesome, but that is such a small percentage of what the athlete needs to go through to make that happen. They have to lift weights, eat healthy, practice, study film, etc. - many things outside of actually playing the game - but these unpleasant tasks make them into a champion. Being a champion in anything is "freaking awesome!"

Comedians are another example. I'm sure some think they're funny and could be a stand up comedian. But it takes a lot of work. It may take months coming up with thirty minutes of solid material, and that is just the content. Delivery is

Become the Ace

everything in comedy. It may take weeks of rehearsing over and over to get it right. Going on stage and being hilarious is awesome, but few are willing to put in the work to make that happen.

5. Are you willing to try green eggs and ham?

I've noticed that sprinkling in humor once in awhile has made me more effective at influencing others. If people are still searching for their purpose, I've always had fun asking this question because it's unusual compared to what I talk about most of the time. I normally ask thought provoking questions and quote great people, like Martin Luther King, Jr, Gandhi, and Eleanor Roosevelt.

Sometimes you can get a powerful message in unexpected places. Spoiler alert! Skip this paragraph if you haven't read the classic *Green Eggs and Ham* by Dr. Seuss. Sam-I-Am offers green eggs and ham to another character throughout the book who is resistant to trying it. After Sam-I-Am's constant nagging he gives in and tries it. He is amazed to find out he loves it and thanks Sam-I-Am.

Become the Ace

This children's book shows us the power of having an open mind. If you aren't sure what you want to do with your life, go out and explore. Try new things. Your greatest talent may emerge from something you never considered.

Green Eggs and Ham has a deeper message. Many say *Green Eggs and Ham* represents accepting God into your life. Faith has changed many lives, but you can also look at it this in another way.

The story also makes me think of a quote from Steve Job's commencement speech he delivered at Stanford: "Don't let the noise of other's opinions drown out your inner voice. And most important, have the courage to follow your heart and intuition."

Sam-I-Am can represent your heart and intuition. There may be times you know what you're supposed to do but you're resistant because you worry about failing or what others think. Be courageous! The world needs you. You can look at problems at an angle that only *you* can see and come up with solutions that only *you* can think of.

Become the Ace

Your calling may not come to you immediately. It's disappointing to say this, but you have to be patient. Also, you'll know when you find your purpose. You'll feel it.

6. Do you realize you're enough right now?

That's great if you want to be an Ace, but don't wait until you become an Ace to be happy. If you're a "two" now, be content with it while believing in your heart you'll be an Ace someday. Realize you're enough while on the pursuit of becoming an Ace. One story back from high school highlights this.

Before Facebook and all of these other social media platforms I don't keep up with, there was Myspace. My friend Adam and I used it to talk to girls. I don't remember whose idea this was, but we both started emailing every girl and asked them what they rated us on a scale of 1 to 10.

We got a large enough sample size to know our numbers. I was about a 6. Adam was about a 9.5. It wasn't even close. I can admit Adam was better looking than me. One girl gave Adam a 10 and he asked her out. Not only did she say yes, but Adam

Become the Ace

even got one of her friends to go out with me. *Awesome, right?*

I drove over to his house so we could meet them in his car because we both agreed that my car wasn't exactly a "chick magnet." I was nervous, but Adam was *really* nervous. He had a pimple on the left side of his face you could barely see and was freaking out.

I told him, "I don't even see it. Let it go. I don't even know why you're nervous. She thinks you're a 10. How do you think the girl that's my date is going to feel when she gets me instead of you?"

Adam replied, "With this pimple I'm *only* a 9.5."

I will always remember that line. I didn't know it at the time, but as good looking as my friend was he felt he wasn't good looking enough. I could never imagine saying, "I'm only a 9.5." This helped me realize it doesn't matter how successful you become if you keep delaying happiness until you reach the next level, or worse, perfection. You're starting on a path of self-destruction.

Become the Ace

I had another good friend, Jason, who was one of the most popular guys in high school. I wanted to switch places with him and every girl wanted to date him. He was thin, about 5'10 and 140 pounds. He came over to my house one day and wasn't himself.

He told me that this guy, Tim, who was a grade higher than him was making fun of him in gym class for being so weak and scrawny. Jason started quizzing me about diet and nutrition. I was 6'3" and 200 pounds at the time and had been lifting weights for several years.

Jason said, "I'm going to get so huge and beat Tim's ass. *No one* will ever call me weak and scrawny again!"

I worked out in my garage, but Jason thought it would be better if we both started going to a local gym. I agreed. Before I started working out with Jason, I believed I worked out hard. I was mistaken. It was because I didn't have the pain my friend had. He often pushed himself so hard he would throw up and even tear up on some sets.

Become the Ace

A year later he was 190 pounds of solid muscle and could bench 315 pounds. All he seemed to care about was getting Tim's approval. He mentioned to me, "I easily benched the most out of all the guys in gym class. Tim could only do 265 pounds, that's pathetic."

Jason never lost his drive for lifting weights. We started going to the gym during junior year and at graduation he was now 6 foot even, 215 pounds with 5% body fat. It was really impressive. Fortunately, now my friend has a healthy mindset and is over seeking Tim's approval.

He dreams of becoming a professional body builder because he loves how it pushes him mentally and physically. We're over five years removed from high school and last time we got together he was 250 pounds of solid muscle and could bench 500 pounds!

I even brought up, "Do you remember being impressed with how I was built in high school? You were so impressed I could bench 250 pounds and back then I weighed 70 pounds more than you.

Become the Ace

Look at us now. You now weigh 70 pounds more than me and can bench twice what I do."

I've realized a burning desire to achieve something the way my friend had usually comes from pain. Avoiding pain, at times, is a better motivator than gaining pleasure. It's best to pursue a dream because it's what you love and you want to share your gift with the world, however, if your burning desire comes from being hurt, trying to prove people wrong is a problem.

I've found forgiveness to be the key to getting over it. A lot of us naturally do that over time. People are going to hurt you in your life. It's because they're hurting. Find the strength to let it go and always realize you're enough in the present moment while pursuing your dream.

What initially made Jason successful was the loss of love he experienced. You'll never truly be successful if you don't realize you're enough in the present moment. You can become fit and make a lot of money, but until you realize you're always enough you *cannot* live the dream.

Become the Ace

Trying to prove people wrong is a great motivator, but it should never be the main motivation behind your dream. I'll mention Earl Nightingale's definition of success again here, "Success is the progressive realization of a worthy ideal." Working to achieve something purely out of acceptance is *not* a worthy ideal.

I know several guys who post shirtless pictures of themselves on a daily basis. I did this years ago and now realize it was because I had low self-worth. I needed confirmation from others to feel good.

If you ask why people are bragging and telling the world about their accomplishments they will likely tell you they are proud of all their hard work. That's great. However, at a certain point, the approval you give yourself *has* to be enough. What others think will always be out of your control and there may be times you won't get that love and acceptance from others you were hoping for.

Your opinion *has* to be enough. It is the only guaranteed way to keep moving closer to your dream. Once you realize you're enough and always will be, you can then focus on your purpose. Your

Become the Ace

purpose should always involve others and something larger than yourself.

Chapter 3

Risk

"If you are not willing to risk the unusual, you will
have to settle for the ordinary."

—Jim Rohn

Becoming An ace will involve taking Ace level risk.

Many say they would be willing to take a risk and
live a better life, but *not* today. It always seems to be

Become the Ace

"someday," a day that never comes. This is especially true when you are young. You think you have so much time that you can afford to wait for the perfect opportunity to start taking risks.

Why do dreams go unlived? The fear of failure, fear of criticism, fear of uncertainty, and the fear of losing connection, among other fears. These are normal fears, but you can change how you view these by prioritizing what's most important in life.

Making serving others your top priority limits risk and allows you to take action.

Oftentimes, you don't take risk for fear of damaging our ego or because others will think less of you. If you agree with this it's time to hear about the "Pratfall Effect"

The Pratfall Effect states that an individual's perceived attractiveness increases or decreases after he or she makes a mistake. If you're striving to become an Ace in life, striving to be perfect can harm you (2).

This phenomenon was first described by social psychologist Elliot Aronson in 1966. Aronson conducted an experiment by testing likability of two individuals that were both perceived as competent. One subject spilled coffee on himself and the other didn't.

The one that spilled the coffee was perceived as being more likeable(3). Making mistakes is something we all do, so if you see someone making a mistake, you connect with them and they are perceived to be more likable.

Now it should make sense why every magazine at check out highlights on the mistakes celebrities are making. It's because most of us don't know what it's like to be rich and famous. Finding their faults brings them "down to earth."

My point is, embrace your mistakes and imperfections. Be willing to take risks. If you happen to fail, people generally will console you, not say things along the lines of, "I told you so." Odds are you'll succeed, but if you're met with temporary defeat, let your improved likability from the "Pratfall effect" help you make the necessary adjustments to succeed in the future.

Become the Ace

You've heard often that you have to take a "leap of faith." Is it true 100% of the time? No. Sometimes your risk involves other people and other obligations, like debt. I loved author Jeff Goins' idea of building a bridge to your calling from his bestselling book *The Art of Work*. He writes, "Discovering your calling is not an epiphany but a series of intentional decisions. It looks less like a giant leap and more like a building a bridge."

Building a bridge can also be known as a "side hustle." There are many obstacles that can get in the way of your dreams. Sometimes it's that your full-time job is draining and you need to spend your off time recovering. Other times it's your bills or obligations you have to your family.

Your circumstances may be difficult, but don't give up on your dream. You can always be doing *something*. Maybe you're thinking, "There are people out there that are putting 60 plus hours a week at this, how will I ever be able to compete with them?"

You can actually use your lack of time to your advantage. More time *doesn't* always mean more production. This is where Parkinson's law applies. The law states: work expands so as to fill the time available for its completion.

My least productive week this past year was when I was on vacation from my pharmacy job. Despite my full-time job, I was consistently putting thirty to forty hours a week into writing and speaking. I was excited about this week off. I thought I would put eighty hours towards my dream.

What actually happened? I was unproductive. I was lacking the sense of urgency I normally had when working my regular job. I was checking email and Facebook every fifteen minutes, texting, and thinking about what I should be doing instead of actually doing it.

This law applies to everyone. Writing an English paper can be done in a day, but you're often given a couple weeks to finish it. It usually gets done the night before. My point is, if you feel you can't take the leap of faith right now, that doesn't mean you can't be building a bridge now so the jump you take in the future is less of a risk.

Become the Ace

Steve Harvey helped me realized that at some point you have to jump to be successful. You can take your time and make a calculated risk, but eventually risk will be involved. Click the link below to a six minute video he did. It will inspire you to take more risks in your life. I suggest watching it multiple times to let his message sink in.

You Gotta Jump to Be Successful

The late motivational speaker, Zig Ziglar "jumped." No one wanted to publish his book, _See You at the Top_ so he decided to take a risk and order 25,000 copies himself. When he started writing the book he was thirty-seven pounds overweight, but he set a goal of completing the book in ten months while simultaneously losing all of that extra weight.

He took a risk on himself and it paid off. The book has sold millions of copies and Zig Ziglar is considered one of the greatest motivational speakers of all time. What if you don't have that strong belief in yourself? Is there still hope if you feel this way? Yes!

Quitting your day job and pursuing your dream is a big jump. You don't have to do this today, but you

Become the Ace

need to start taking smaller jumps. Announcing to people what you want to do is the first step.

Odds are the first people you tell about what you want to do will laugh and tell you to be more realistic. Do you think anyone on their deathbed says, "I've made many mistakes, but I'm glad I was realistic." No!

Realistic is boring. Realistic is not fulfilling. Realistic is not why you're on this earth. I fantasize often about everyone on this earth acquiring the right mindset and values and living fulfilling lives, but it's not going to happen.

There is one big selling point on being realistic. It provides certainty. I've found a majority would rather live an unpleasant life and be certain about their future than live an adventure and be uncertain. With uncertainty comes risk.

You can limit risk by taking a moment to think about what's really at stake. A lot of times you don't take risks or get out of your comfort zone because you worry about damaging your ego and reputation.

Become the Ace

But you need to always be operating in a state of mind of who you want to *become* not who you currently *are*. When you do this, all failure becomes feedback which allows you to make the adjustments to become who you want to be even faster. It's possible you'll make a fool of yourself from time to time by taking risks, but you'll look at it differently if you're always looking forward.

You'll say, "I'll look back at this and laugh," or "I'm glad I took that risk. It didn't work out, but I gained valuable insight that set me up for my future success."

Tony Robbins has stated, "The quality of your life is in direct proportion to the amount of uncertainty you can comfortably deal with." We've all heard the saying: "No risk, no reward."

However, you can take small jumps by taking calculated risks and with each successful jump you can build that certainty to take the leap of faith one day.

Chapter 4

———◦———

Deliberate Practice

"We're talkin' bout practice. We ain't talking about
the game. We're talkin' bout practice, man."

— Allen Iverson

Most sports fans remember this rant on practice
Allen Iverson had in 2002. Iverson's team,
The Philadelphia 76ers, had been eliminated from
the playoffs four days prior. His coach at the time,
Larry Brown, questioned his work ethic. He said,

Become the Ace

"Iverson has 'got to change,' that he 'has to be practicing, he has to set the example'." Brown also mentioned players "simply won't be here" if they aren't "responsible enough and sensitive enough to their teammates to be on time, to practice, to prepare."(4)

Be honest. Do you have fun practicing? I know I didn't. I played one sport in high school - golf. I was one of the worst on the team. I had days where I shot near even par, but my handicap was somewhere around fifteen.

I had no desire to spend hours at the driving range or practice putting. I just wanted to play. It didn't matter how much I played, I didn't get any better. On the other hand, I knew some guys on the team who practiced every day and kept getting better and better. How come they got better and I didn't? Because their practice was deliberate.

I've read multiple times it take 10,000 hours to become an "overnight" success. After some number crunching, I thought that if you spent forty hours a week working on your craft, in five years you would be a master (40 hours per week x 52 weeks a year x 5 years= 10,400 hours).

How awesome is this? You can be a master at your craft in five years. This is still possible, but many fail to realize that not all hours you have done or will do count towards this total. How you're spending your time practicing is far more important than the amount.

One book I got for Christmas in 2015 was *Moonwalking with Einstein* by Joshua Foer. It was a fantastic book. He is a journalist who covered the USA Memory Championship. One of the contestants told him that an average memory, if used properly, could win the event. He gets help from one of the "mental athletes," but as the competition approached he found himself hitting a plateau.

This is the time he learned from Dr. K. Anders Ericsson, who is a psychologist at Florida State University where the acquisition of expert performance and deliberate practice is one of his main areas of research.

Become the Ace

Here's something interesting I found after looking at Dr. Ericsson's published work.

Significant improvements in performance were realized when individuals were

1. Given a task with a well-defined goal
2. Motivated to improve
3. Provided with feedback
4. Provided with ample opportunities for repetition and gradual refinements of their performance.

Deliberate efforts to improve performance on a skill requires full concentration and often requires problem-solving and better methods of performing the tasks. (12)

Whatever your skill you're trying to develop, are you honestly using these four steps? Are you using the part of your brain involved in critical thinking (prefrontal cortex) or are you using the emotional part (limbic system)?

I'm honest with myself. There have been several times growing up where I had no defined goals. I was just going with the flow. I was not motivated to

Become the Ace

improve. I was content where I was and didn't want to try and improve because I didn't want to be disappointed. I avoided feedback and called those giving me tough love (also known as constructive criticism) "haters." And, lastly, I did not put myself in opportunities for repetition and gradual refinements because it wasn't fun.

However, there was one time I did engage in deliberate practice as a teenager and realized it on my way home from work recently.

It was with kissing. That's right, kissing. The story begins in 11th grade English class, taught by Mrs. Miller. I *never* talked, which is why I never had a date. I've always hated English, but this class was different. It was because of who sat next to me. Her name was Sarah.

Let's just say she was very easy on the eyes. *It would be great if I could go out with a girl like her, but that could only happen in my dreams*, I thought. However, one day she asked for my phone, put her number in it and asked me to text her. *Is this a joke?*

After an afternoon of texting, she asked me if I wanted to go see a movie with her. *Of course!* It still

44

Become the Ace

didn't make sense to me why a girl like Sarah wanted to go out with me, but I didn't have time to overthink the situation.

I assumed I'd have to see a chick flick like the *Notebook,* but it was a small price to pay. I assumed wrong. She said we could see whatever I wanted. We saw *Semi-Pro* starring one of America's gems, Will Ferrell.

It never occurred to me that I probably could have gotten my first kiss during the movie, that had an audience of five people, until *after* the movie was over. I was clueless when it came to women at that point in my life (who am I kidding? I'm still clueless.)

Despite my cluelessness, I knew that once we got in my car, a 1995 Green Mercury Sable - a total chick magnet, it was time to kiss Sarah. As I was sitting there slightly hyperventilating, with a heart rate in the triple digits, I started a conversation with myself.

Just kiss her already. No. Don't do that. You have no idea what you're doing. You're going to make an idiot of yourself and she's going to tell the whole school how lame

Become the Ace

your are. This back in forth went on for a few more seconds before I decided to be honest with Sarah.

"It's embarrassing, but this is my first date and I've never kissed a girl before," I said with shame. She smiled, moved closer to me and replied, "That's adorable." A few seconds later she kissed me. It lasted about five seconds and I remember thinking, *This is awesome! I finally kissed a girl. One less thing my friends can tease me about.*

Sarah backed away and paused a few seconds before saying, "You need to work on kissing. That was pretty bad." That brought me from proud to humiliated quickly. My head sagged and I didn't want to look at her.

But then I picked up my head and put on a smile. I replied in a confident, smooth voice, "I guess that means I need some practice. What do you think?"

I went from using the emotional part of my brain (feeling embarrassed, worrying about what other kids at school would think if Sarah told people) to the cognitive (deliberate practice).

Become the Ace

When it came to becoming a better kisser, I used Dr. Ericsson's four steps to developing a skill:

1) Given a task with a well-defined goal

Task: Become a better kisser

Goal: Never get a negative comment about my kissing skills ever again

2) Motivated to improve

I was 17 years old and what others thought about me was everything. I did not want a rumor spread around school about how awful I was.

3) Provided with feedback

Sarah gave me lots of feedback. I learned three things right a way:

1. When I kiss I should have my eyes closed. Apparently, "creepy weirdos" kiss with their eyes open.
2. I was moving my tongue around too fast. I needed to slow it down.
3. I was making too much noise

Become the Ace

She also pointed out what she liked and encouraged me to keep doing it.

4) Provided with ample opportunities for repetition and gradual refinements of their performance.

We practiced for an hour during our first date and I was over at her house every afternoon after school for a week straight.

I put my ego and emotions aside and focused on deliberate practice. A week later, Sarah told me, "Michael. You know what? You're a good kisser now." Maybe that moment wasn't the proudest moment of my life, but it has to be at least in the top five.

My relationship with Sarah was short-lived, but as we broke up I made sure to thank her for helping me with my kissing. Overall, the response I've received from other girls throughout the years about my kissing has been at worst, neutral.

I want to point out that Sarah was the only girl that I've kissed where I've used these four steps. Isn't that what happens with most of your skills? You get

Become the Ace

to a point where you are good and decide that's enough.

It's possible I could be the best kisser in the world if kept my deliberate practice up. That's why few master a skill. You have to *love* what you're doing. Deliberate practice is often boring and tedious. Plus the better you get, the harder it is to improve. At that point you have to dig deep, get uncomfortable, and push through limits you think are impossible.

It's tough finding the motivation when no one is forcing you to master your skill. It's human nature to not do something if you don't have to. I think about checking out at Walmart. Every time I'm in there I notice a big line with a cashier and the self-checkout is always open.

A majority think, "I have a cashier to ring my stuff up. Why would I do it myself?" You're different. You want to put in that little extra effort because you want an amazing, fulfilling life. Your time is valuable and you don't want to waste a second of it. Deliberate practice is a sure-fire way to make sure you're using your time wisely.

Become the Ace

You *have* to be getting better or you're wasting your time. Why do something that's boring and tedious for nothing? If you're not committed to deliberate practice just watch Netflix. I know from personal experience it's easy to spent a whole day binge watching amazing shows.

It's easy to get discouraged and give up. It's easy to acquire a mindset of never being good enough and always needing to get better. It can be draining…if you let it.

Look at your dream in the active tense. By doing what you love you are *living* the dream, not the past tense (you've *lived* the dream). Look at yourself as a masterpiece that you'll spend your whole life working on. You are a never-ending work in progress.

Looking at it this way helps you become more analytical and less emotional when it comes to working on your craft. You'll get over negative criticism fast. Let's say someone says that you're awful. If you don't respect their opinion, ignore them. However, if you do, ask them why they think

Become the Ace

so. Take their advice constructively and use it to your advantage.

You're human, and you're going to get embarrassed at times. I recall how I felt after Sarah told me, "You need to work on kissing. That was pretty bad." But you don't want to throw a pity party. From my experience they have low attendance rates and those that do attend never have fun.

Remember, you are an ongoing work in progress and there is no limit on what you can do with the skill you choose to develop. You can make an effort to be deliberate in most areas of my life. You can strive to be a better spouse, friend, employee, father or mother, son or daughter, etc.

You don't want to be a perfectionist, but you also want to never stop growing. You'll love the rush of dopamine you get from improving yourself, no matter how small the improvement, *if* you have the right mindset.

To quote Allen Iverson again, "We're talkin' bout practice. We ain't talking about the game. We're talking about practice, man." However, now you know if it's the *right* kind of practice you can kiss

Become the Ace

failure goodbye and start walking on the path to becoming an "overnight" success.

Chapter 5

Taking Action

"Action is the foundational key to all success."

— Pablo Picasso

Inaction stops you from living your dreams. A friend recently told me: "Youth is for the wasteful." It's true. When we're in our 20s is the time to take action and take risks. Why doesn't this happen for many of us? Because you feel there is so much time. The truth is you never know how much

Become the Ace

time you have. That's why the right time is always *now*.

Sometimes you have to just do the "Macarena." The song that was a hit in the early 90's by Los del Rio and the song that plays at every wedding? Yes. Let me explain. I've always loved that song and wanted to dance to it, but I never danced because I was worried about embarrassing myself.

The "Macarena" was playing during my brother's wedding in 2014. There weren't a lot of people in attendance (about forty people), but almost everyone got up to dance to that song. My table had eight people and I was the only one still sitting. Many were calling me over and encouraging me to do the dance, but I was paralyzed in fear.

I started moving my feet to the music under the table and thought there was a chance I'd go on the floor and dance. But it never happened. The following day I was disappointed that I didn't dance. I even downloaded the song on my iPod and was dancing to it alone in my bedroom. This didn't help. It wasn't the same.

Become the Ace

Half the people were drunk anyway. Why didn't I take action and dance? A year later I was able to attend a friend's wedding and told myself, "I have to dance to the Macarena. It's a fever that only dancing will relieve." I honestly believed that if it played, I was going to dance to it, but shockingly the song never came on.

I was at a wedding. I was in the right environment to get what I wanted, but it didn't happen. *Why couldn't I just dance at my brother's wedding when I had the chance? What if I never get to dance to the "Macarena" ever again?*

This story should teach you to take action. At the next wedding I attend I'm going to ask the DJ to play the "Macarena" and I'll be the first one to start dancing to it. I don't care if I make a fool of myself. Half the people will be drunk anyway.

The "Macarena" should be a metaphor for what you want to do in your life but you're delaying for some reason. Fear of failure? Fear of criticism? Waiting for the perfect moment? Everyone does this. However, getting in the habit of taking action will be a huge advantage for you.

Become the Ace

It's possible you're a victim of the "Spotlight Effect." The Spotlight Effect a term in psychology that refers to our tendency to think that other people are watching us more closely than they actually are (5). My friend who said he was "only a 9.5" experienced this in the chapter on desire because of the pimple he had on his face.

I'm sure you have been at an awards ceremony or graduation where someone fell on their face as they walked on stage. I'm sure they felt embarrassed, but the event was easily forgotten. Plus, most people were probably wondering if they were okay instead of laughing at them.

People in general focus on themselves more than anyone else. Dale Carnegie asked his readers in the book *How to Win Friends and Influence People,* who was the first person they looked at in a group photo. They admitted they looked at themselves first. You probably look at yourself first - I do too. This should remind you that people focus on themselves more than you, and you should never let fear of embarrassing yourself prevent you from taking action.

Become the Ace

We are all different. Maybe fear of embarrassing yourself is not what stops you from taking action. Maybe it's a perfectionist nature. Many have this issue, or at the very least, use it as an excuse to not take action.

Ever say the following?

1. "If I'm going to do it, I want to do it right. I want to be one hundred percent invested."

This could be a problem. What if you have a full-time job and family obligations? If you say you are waiting until you quit your job to work on achieving your dream, it's not going to happen. I've seen this often with people wanting to go back to school.

They say if they go back to school, they want to be a full-time student. I know taking just one class per semester to get a degree may take you a lot longer, but at least you're taking action. It doesn't matter how slow you're going, it will *always* be better than doing nothing. Sometimes you'll need to make your dream a side-hustle for a brief period before you can do it full-time.

Become the Ace

2. "I can't attend every meeting so there's no point."

I've done this with attending church. I work every other Sunday and could only attend half the time. I used this same excuse to not join Toastmasters, a speaking organization, for over a year for the same reason.

I honestly believed that if you don't go every week there's no point. Have you ever felt this way? I realize now how wrong this is. Maybe it will take you twice as long, but great things take time. Again, something is *always* better than nothing. Do what you can.

You never know what the future holds for you. You may be presented with a life changing opportunity and by making an effort to take immediate action, despite not being able to make it one hundred percent of the time, could be the difference from you being prepared or not.

3. "I need to be perfect. I'm not doing it until then."

Perfection doesn't exist, but many times you stop yourself from taking action until you are at a high level. There's nothing wrong with having a high

Become the Ace

standard for what you do. But look at it this way: if you engage in deliberate practice, your best work will *always* be ahead of you.

Plus, if you're just getting started on the path to your dream you're likely going to be awful. Use this to your advantage. If you're awful, you'll make a lot of mistakes and will be able to learn from them.

Something I learned from Derek Halpern, a successful online business owner and founder of _Social Triggers_, was to get it done, *then* get it perfect. It's always better to take initiative and at least attempt to create something instead of keeping your idea to yourself.

I'm not saying put out total crap, but I am saying do the best you can in the present moment and always take relentless action. You'll probably fail and fail often. Failure will always be part of being successful and achieving your dream.

Action is crucial. It's even more important than a great idea. I just recently read _The 4-Hour Workweek_, by Tim Ferriss, which is one of my favorite books.

Become the Ace

I recently read an article where Ferriss was being interviewed titled, "Trust Me Your Idea is Worthless" where I found this insightful answer that highlights the importance of execution and action:

"Almost anyone can (and has!) come up with a great idea, but only a skilled entrepreneur can execute it. Skilled in this case doesn't mean experienced; it means flexible and **action-oriented**, someone who recognizes that mistakes can often be corrected, but time lost postponing a decision is lost forever. Ideas, however necessary, are not sufficient. They are just an entry ticket to play the game."(6)

Planning can make a world of a difference. It can get you to your ultimate destination faster. But without action, you'll always be stuck where you currently are. You have what it takes to be an Ace, but it will require action, and lots of it.

I'll end this chapter by talking about the best way to take action: thinking about how it affects others. Whenever you are doing something that is larger than yourself your motivation goes up and your procrastination goes down.

Become the Ace

Maybe you feel you are limited, but if you can take action and make something of yourself it can give others hope and an excellent role model to follow. Or maybe you strongly believe in what you're doing and know it will make a difference for people.

The Civil Rights Movement is a perfect example. There were so many brave men and women who risked their lives to improve the lives of their sons and daughters and future generations. Often people need a reference on how to become an Ace.

If you can get in the habit of taking immediate action and putting in all the work it takes to do something great, it will no doubt make a positive impact on people currently living and future generations.

Say to yourself, "I'm doing it for them." You can even do this for goals that only affect you. Imagine your future self. Picture yourself a year out, five years out, ten years out, and on your deathbed. Think about the pain your current inaction is doing to your future self. This can help you develop discipline. Jim Rohn has said, "The pain of

Become the Ace

discipline weighs ounces, the pain of regret weighs tons."

Every time you put something off that you know you should be doing, it causes your future self a lot of pain. That's what developing discipline is all about; it involves putting off immediate gratification and comfort in the present in favor of a better future and an improved version of yourself.

It doesn't matter if your goals only benefit you, or if they are something larger and involve many others. Whenever you are feeling unmotivated or you're afraid, say to yourself, "I'm doing it for them." It doesn't matter who "they" are, when you're doing something to benefit someone else, your life has more meaning and you find the strength to do things you never thought you could do.

Chapter 6

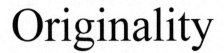

Originality

"Originality is really important."

— Jim Carrey

Well, there you have it. Jim Carrey said originality is important and you should believe it too. It doesn't matter what you achieve in life, if you do it by not being your true self then you've failed. Deep down everyone is good person and can do something memorable with their life.

Become the Ace

But trying to please everyone and be accepted often prevents them from being proud of who they are.

It's human nature to want to be liked. One of our needs is a feeling of love and belonging, but you won't get to truly experience it if you can't be yourself. Look at yourself as a meal. Always put being nutritious ahead of being delicious. Let me explain.

Years ago, I wanted everyone, to order me for dinner and would have done whatever it took to get more people to the table. I got blonde highlights, wore expensive and uncomfortable clothes, became the "that's what she said guy," and just about anything else I thought I needed to be liked.

I thought if I worked hard enough, that one day I would be able to win *everybody* over. Once I looked at myself as a meal it occurred to me that it isn't possible. Let's say you're throwing a party and can only serve one food. What would you choose?

Pizza seems to be a solid choice. *Everyone* loves pizza right? Most people do, but not everyone. Some are lactose intolerant, some are vegan, and others want something healthier. You can change to

Become the Ace

another dish if you want. You can be grilled chicken and vegetables with your body builder friends, ice cream with those who have a sweet tooth, and hot wings with those that like it spicy.

You can constantly change to please people. You may have done this most of your life. Make a decision to not do it anymore. It's exhausting. It takes too much thinking. I decided I was going to become grilled salmon, with brown rice and steamed broccoli at all times.

You would be more popular if you were a slice of pepperoni pizza, but it's not nutritious. A healthy meal is the best thing for you, but most don't want what's best for them. Most want instant gratification of something greasy and fattening hitting their tastebuds. They're not focused on what it's doing to their health.

The key to being your authentic self if to separate what you achieve from who you are. Who you are, what makes you "nutritious," represents your beliefs and values.

Choose to be nutritious at all times, but do it in a way that is healthy for yourself and others. Again,

Become the Ace

deep down everyone is nutritious, but nutritious isn't as appealing as delicious. That's why being true to who you are is difficult.

Being real may be the most challenging part of life. All it takes is one thing for you to start doubting yourself, to start feeling inferior, and start looking to fix what's not broken. Staying true to who you are will be an ongoing challenge for the rest of your life.

Oftentimes, you'll direct all your attention to pleasing the one person who hates you, instead of the *dozens* who already love you. Oftentimes, you'll direct all your attention to correcting a weakness and by doing so, weakening your strengths.

This happened to me in little league baseball. I pitched. One season our team had the best record in an eight team league. The pitchers that had the most wins were myself and a girl named Julie.

I did not throw the ball hard at all. In fact, Julie threw *much* harder and it wasn't even close. But I could consistently throw strikes and that's what helped our team win. Our team won the first two rounds of the playoffs and our next game was the

Become the Ace

championship. The coach decided to have me start the game.

Before the game started, I was warming up at the mound and was feeling great. If I could carry this feeling into the game our team would have a solid chance of taking home the trophy. Then I let one comment get to me - "Look at this wuss on the mound. There's a girl on his team and she throws harder than him." This came from a kid on the other team and after he said this, most of the other team was laughing at me.

I couldn't let it go. I stopped caring about being accurate and instead was throwing the ball as hard as I could. I was wild. I could no longer throw strikes. It was by far the worst game of my life. After a couple of innings the other team was so far ahead that there was no way we could come back.

I was a chubby, quiet kid at that time, and pitching well gave me confidence I was lacking. Playing baseball was my favorite thing in the world, but that championship game was my last game. The coach picked me to pitch over Julie and I let him

Become the Ace

down. I let my team down. I was in tears at the end of the game and told everyone how sorry I was.

Everyone was supportive, telling me that it's just a game and to forget about it. It would be over a decade before I'd let it go and seek to learn something. It's clear what happened. Even though I was a good pitcher I didn't fit the mold of what a good pitcher looks like to one person.

Instead of being myself and playing to my strength of being accurate, I shifted my focus to what mattered to someone else - throwing the ball hard. I let one comment shatter my confidence and take away what made me good in the first place. Plus, I let this comment cost our team a chance at winning the championship.

I'm sure you've had a similar event in your life. I know Ted Mosby did on the popular show *How I Met Your Mother*. Ted Mosby, played by Josh Radnor, is an architect and later on in the show he begins teaching architecture at a university.

Students love him and he enjoys teaching. He's confident and he's real when in front of the class. His friend Marshall Eriksen, played by Jason Segel,

Become the Ace

suggests he check out a site that students use to rate their professor.

Ted loves what he sees initially. He sees the comments of "funny," "sexy," and "witty puns," and you can tell he feels incredible. *But,* several dozen positive ratings can't overcome the *one* negative one. Someone left the comment "boring." He couldn't let it go. He was bummed out for the rest of the episode.

He starts to second guess himself when he's in front of the class. He stops being himself and, because of this, he actually *does* become boring. It was one of my favorite episodes because it teaches you that you have to be yourself and find a way to get over it when someone rejects you.

Your little quirks and imperfections are what make you unique; they are what makes you an Ace like no other. You're human. You're wired for connection and when someone doesn't give it to you, you tend to focus on how to get it.

You need to be careful, though. Some people spend their whole life chasing the approval of people who will never give it to them. Their reasons for rejecting

Become the Ace

you may be outrageous and something you can do little about.

I think of the movie *Step Brothers* here. Actor Rob Riggles' character explains to Will Ferrell's character that he wants to like him, but he can't. There's something about his face. "If you don't change your face, I'm going to change it for you," he states.

You can spend your whole life making more money, changing the way you look, talk, and act, but every time you go against who you are, and the values you hold, you are paying a price. Your happiness.

You will never be truly happy until you can be yourself. If a girl throws harder than you, who cares? If one of your students finds you boring, it doesn't matter. If someone says you need to fix your face, laugh it off. The only way to be an Ace on the outside is stay an Ace on the inside no matter what. You do this by being yourself. I promise my friend, you're an Ace just the way you are!

That sounds nice, doesn't it? Many of us hear this and agree, but it usually takes awhile before you fully accept it. The love that you need to seek has to

Become the Ace

come from people who love you for who you are, your beliefs, values, and personality. If you try to attract it from what you achieve, how you look, or anything else on the outside, you'll never know for sure if the love is real.

The movie *Coming to America* starring Eddie Murphy, Arsenio Hall, and James Earl Jones resonates with the previous paragraph. If you haven't seen it, I highly recommend you check it out.

Eddie Murphy's character in the film, Akeem Joffer, seems to have the life everyone dreams of. He's wealthy and has servants that do everything for him. His parents have picked out a bride for him, a beautiful woman he's never met and who has been trained to obey Akeem's every command.

Akeem has the awareness to know there's more to life than this. He wants a woman who thinks for herself. He wants a woman he loves and respects. He also wants her to love him for *who he is* and *not* for his wealth and royalty status.

He decides to go to America with his friend Semmi, played by Arsenio Hall. Akeem finds the most run-

Become the Ace

down place he can and takes a job as a custodian at a fast food restaurant. This is his strategy for finding a woman that loves him for who he is.

No one understands why he's doing this. I personally failed to understand it all of the times I watched it growing up. The movie is an accurate representation of what happens in life. Most are focused on what's on the outside. However, it's only until you separate yourself from your status and material possessions that you find out for sure if people love you for who you are.

Being yourself may be the most frightening thing you can do. You may not be the most popular, but you will find people who love you just the way you are. Have faith. People are drawn to others that are authentic to who they are.

Chapter 7

Awareness

"Having awareness of yourself and your
surroundings is a crucial part of living a
fulfilling life."

— Michael Unks

W ho? Wait, that's the guy who wrote this book.
Really? He's quoting himself? Who does he
think he is?

Become the Ace

I'm making a point. I'm aware how others would perceive me for quoting myself. You should be real and live an authentic life, but sometimes you'll have to make changes if you are being perceived differently that how you want to be seen.

One of my favorite shows, *The Office,* starring Steve Carell comes to mind here. His character, Michael Scott, is setting up an online dating profile. He explains that he is looking to become a father and likes kids, so he decides to make his screen name "little kid lover." It's easy to perceive that name differently than what he intended.

Awareness of how you're perceived is crucial. I was shocked when my dad told me that the swastika was originally a Buddhist symbol for peace. Hitler choose that symbol because it meant love and purity. Imagine if you started wearing a swastika on all your clothes. Your reason is because it's a Buddhist symbol that represents love and purity. You will likely be perceived differently.

It's challenging being misinterpreted, but unfortunately, it will always be part of your life. You have all the facts and you know the truth about

Become the Ace

yourself. Others don't. You may compliment and show love to just about everyone you come in contact with. It may look like you're flirting with everyone. People may think, "he or she wants something from me" or "he or she is trying to sell me something," but you may just be trying to make the person feel good about themselves and make them smile.

It can't be avoided though. If you're a guy and say something nice to a woman your age, they're likely going to assume you're looking for a date. A handful of times this past year I've given a woman a compliment just to make her feel good. I wasn't looking for a date or anything in return. However, I heard "I have a boyfriend," and "I'm not interested."

It can be frustrating at times trying to be nice but people think you have an ulterior motive. That's how life is. It's human nature to generalize. I've noticed that it's difficult for people to see someone being nice or giving without expecting something in return.

Become the Ace

I know it's extra work, but it's worth it not to generalize. It's worth it to give a person the benefit of the doubt. Maybe you're at work and a co-worker or customer snaps at you, or someone cuts you off while driving.

It's easy to say, "that guy's a jerk," when the truth is he is just having a bad day or has something stressful going on in his life like a divorce or illness.

I know from personal experience it's easier to forgive and stay positive when people are being negative, bitter, and selfish because of circumstances instead of it being part of who they actually are.

Avoiding generalization will be an important part of maintaining a positive attitude while in pursuit of becoming an Ace. Give people a break so others will give you a break.

Also realize that when someone lashes out at you it often has something to do with them. Focus on your success. When you're successful, some may try to tear you down because they don't like the way it makes them feel.

Become the Ace

Don't take it personally. Everyone has done it. Ever see someone who seems to be younger, less intelligent, and with less talent, but have more success than you? It's because they are working hard and have a proper mindset, but it's much easier to say they got lucky. It's easier to say they got an opportunity that you didn't, have connections, that life isn't fair, etc.

People love when successful people fail. Look at all the magazines that feature celebrities on the cover. It's rarely anything positive. It's mostly about all the mistakes they're making. What do people do when they see a world class athlete who is breaking records? They do their best to uncover him as a fraud. They have to be cheating. Instead of doing things like this, it would be better just to focus on improving yourself on a daily basis and finding a way to succeed despite your shortcomings.

As a general rule, give everyone a break and respect what they have to say. If you're doing something important with your life, it will involve other people. Be willing to listen to how you're being perceived. If you have to make changes, then make them. However, sometimes you have to be willing

Become the Ace

to be misunderstood to become an Ace and you'll have to learn to live with that.

This chapter so far has focused on how you can be perceived and how it does play a factor in how you live your life. Now it's time to focus on self-awareness. We are complex creatures. We are constantly changing. That's why we need to constantly assess why we do what we do.

Bryan Cranston's character Walter White from the mega-hit show *Breaking Bad* is a an example. If you haven't seen it yet, you may want to put this book down and start watching it. It's *that good*.

He starts making meth out of good intentions. He discovers he has lung cancer and wants to make money to support his family after he dies. However, Walter White changes throughout the show. Near the end he accumulates more than enough money to support his family, but keeps making meth because of how powerful it makes him feel.

Near the end he was no longer altruistic and thinking about his family. It was more about becoming significant. In the beginning he's a hero

Become the Ace

that you root for, but that changes as the show goes on.

Walter White shows the value in taking time to evaluate yourself. Some questions he could have asked himself were: "Am I drunk with power?" "I've made enough money. Why am I still doing this?" "Am I doing this because my life hasn't amounted to much and this is a way to go out being significant?"

Self-analysis is often difficult and makes us uncomfortable, but it's worth it to know why you do what you do. It leads to true freedom. Maybe you think you have it all together when you really don't. I've learned this from the TED talk phenomenon, and bestselling author, Dr. Brene Brown.

She has an excellent grasp of human behavior and is an expert on "wholehearted living," but she still continues to see a therapist. Things still bother her, but she doesn't avoid them. She faces them head on and addresses them.

You may not always like why you act and feel the way you do, but if you avoid the truth and never

Become the Ace

deal with it you *can't* be an Ace. Living the dream includes becoming an Ace, but also being content with your current card and doing what you do for the right reasons. This takes awareness.

Chapter 8

———◦———

Refuse to settle

"There is no passion to be found playing small - in settling for a life that is less than the one you are capable of living."

— Nelson Mandela

When you're living the dream you have it all - your life is full of passion, you have amazing family and friends, and you have an incredible work-life balance. You shouldn't have to choose.

Become the Ace

You can find a way to have it all. I learned this the last time I went to a game room I went to often growing up.

I was ten years old when I first went to Dave and Buster's, a restaurant and game room with seventy-three locations throughout the United States. My dad gave my sister and I $20 worth of credit to play any games we wanted and I tried almost everything: Skeeball, basketball, claw machines, and many more. I had spent half of my credit and had few tickets to show for it.

This all changed once I sat down to play a Vegas style slot machine called "Match em up" where you must get triple sevens to hit the jackpot. It spins around in a circle and you press a button trying to hit the 7, and you must land on the 7 to hit the jackpot.

Here's a video of someone playing it: Click here to see "Match em up"

The jackpot was at 500 tickets, which meant that close to a 100 people had played it without hitting the jackpot. The first time I played it I hit the jackpot. I couldn't believe it. I could get a lot of cool

Become the Ace

stuff in the ticket room with 500 tickets, like temporary tattoos, candy necklaces, and a slinky.

I played the game a second time and hit the jackpot again! Tried a third time and same result. I spent the rest of my $10 credit playing that game and found myself hitting the jackpot eighty percent of the time.

A crowd of ten people gathered around the machine because they were amazed at what I was doing. A manager had to come over and add more tickets to the machine because I was hitting the jackpot so much.

Now is a good time to point out that I wasn't gifted at anything *until* I played this game. After I ran out of credit, I saw I almost had enough tickets for a lava lamp, which was 4,500 tickets.

What if I only played Match 'em up the next time we came to Dave and Busters?, I thought. That's exactly what I did. I continued to hit the jackpot eighty percent of the time and every time I played I had a crowd watching. It was great that I was getting so many tickets, but I *wasn't* having fun.

Become the Ace

I would have much rather played basketball or raced motorcycles with my sister, but I had a gift and couldn't waste it. Throughout the years I got some incredible prizes. The prizes included five regular sized lava lamps for 4,500 tickets each, one monster sized lava lamp at 20,000 tickets, and signed Dan Marino framed picture for 25,000 tickets, and my most valuable prize was a Randy Johnson and Curt Schilling signed baseball that was 50,000 tickets.

My sister had a lot more fun than me. She played whatever she wanted and always cashed in her tickets at each trip. Match em up became a job for me and it would often be a handful of trips before I would spend my tickets. The signed baseball took almost ten trips.

I never spent the tickets on anyone else. My main focus was getting attention from people in the gameroom and showing off all the prizes I won. It occurred to me that there was a lesson to be learned here.

I'm human. We all have a need for significance and I loved the attention I was getting from everyone in

Become the Ace

the gameroom. Also, I've been taught that having a lot of tickets is what all kids envy. I could use those tickets to show off the prizes most people could never have.

In life, maybe you have an *actual* talent, not the minor one I had with Match 'em up. Maybe you don't even enjoy it, but you do it because people are amazed to see your gift and you get paid well to do it. Since your talent doesn't bring much satisfaction, you use your money to buy a bunch of things you don't need to make you happy.

Or, maybe you refuse to spend your money like I refused to spend my tickets because you want incredible prizes. This is like waiting until you're retired to enjoy yourself. I approached Dave and Buster's the wrong way. I was supposed to enjoy myself a little more.

Years later I moved from Florida to South Carolina and in South Carolina there weren't any Dave and Buster's. About ten years went by before I back to that Dave and Buster's in Hollywood, Florida.

It looked vastly different, but Match 'em up was in the same place. It took me a couple tries before I hit

Become the Ace

the Jackpot, but then I was back to hitting the jackpot eighty percent of the time. Again, people started to gather around. Nothing had changed. But now I wanted to have more balance in my life.

We were in town for my brother's wedding and after hitting the jackpot about ten times I decided it was time to play games with my family. We played basketball, Skeeball, and all the shooting and racing games. For the first time in my life I enjoyed my experience at Dave and Buster's.

I still hit the jackpot ten times and had a decent amount of tickets, but I decided I wasn't going to spend any on myself. My sister wasn't used to having this many tickets and I let her pick out something she normally never could get.

She got an inflatable *Simpson's* couch for 3,000 tickets. I didn't enjoy playing Match 'em up, but seeing the smile on my sister's face was worth it.

That's when I realized that you don't always have to enjoy what you do to be fulfilled and satisfied. Sometimes you make sacrifices to improve the lives of those you care about. I also learned that you are not on this earth to be a money-making machine.

Become the Ace

It's great to want to save and spend a majority of your time doing tasks that give you a high rate of return, however you need to enjoy yourself, too. My plan growing up was to get a six-figure job, work for decades, retire a multimillionaire, *then* spend my money and start enjoying myself. I would buy prizes the equivalent to the Randy Johnson and Curt Schilling baseball.

There was one problem to this. If you did this, about seventy percent of your life would be behind you and you would have very few memorable experiences because you spent it working and saving. Experiences bring more joy and fulfillment than material possessions.

Spending your hard earned money on others without question brings more satisfaction than spending it on yourself. It's great if you have a gift, but use that gift wisely. Developing and using your gift may not be enjoyable, but allow yourself to step away from it from time to time.

Play Skee Ball and race motorcycles in the "gameroom of life." Save your tickets, but allow yourself to get a candy necklace or two during each

Become the Ace

trip. Use your tickets to improve the quality of life of others and put a smile on their faces.

When you find that balance I found during my last trip to Dave and Buster's, that's when you are really living like an Ace. Refuse to settle. You really can have it all!

Chapter 9

Persistence

"Just because is isn't happening right now doesn't mean it never will."

— Zig Ziglar

Persistence is simply following through on your plan no matter how difficult it is. If you're dreaming big and want to live in abundance, it's possible. It may seem like you have to pick and choose, but you can have it all. You just need to

Become the Ace

follow through! The moment I realized this, sparks literally flew.

Golf has been an incredible way for my dad and I to bond throughout my life. I first went to the golf course with him when I was five years old. I would ride in the golf cart and whenever we got to the green it was my time to start playing. I had a plastic putter and a plastic golf ball and I got to pretend like I was playing just like my dad.

A couple years later I got a *real* set of clubs and got *real* golf balls to play with. For several years I didn't care about how well I was doing, I just liked spending time with my dad and enjoyed being outside.

The way I gripped the club was bizarre. It looked like I was holding a hockey stick when I swung. As years went on, spending time with my dad and enjoying the outdoors wasn't enough. I need to start playing better too. One of my dad's friends said, "If you ever want to be good, you have to change your grip." He showed me the proper way to grip the club and it felt awkward.

Become the Ace

I tried the new grip on the remaining holes and it was the worst round of my life. I was not having fun. I asked my dad for his advice, "Should I go back to my old grip or do you think I should do it the right way?"

The question he asked me would have an impact on how I approached golf, and many other areas of my life. He asked, "Do you want to be good *or* do you want to have fun?" I chose to be good. My dad's friend was right. The grip change eventually did help my game improve.

Being good was top priority now. Bonding with dad and having fun didn't matter. I even became a member of my high school golf team. This caused a lot of stress. I was one of the worst on the team and put a lot of pressure on myself to play well.

There was a radical shift in enjoyment from when I was five years old with plastic clubs and when I was in my twenties. Golf had now become a job. It was no longer an escape. Eventually, I couldn't take it anymore and didn't play at all for several years. My dad continued to offer, but I always played the "I have to study" card. It worked every time.

Become the Ace

But recently I've started to look at my past and evaluate all my mistakes and learn from them. This seemed to be one. My first thought was, *Seems like I made the wrong choice. I don't want to be a professional golfer, I should have chosen to have fun. Maybe bonding with my dad is the reward, not playing like Jordan Spieth.*

I decided to take my dad up on his offer to play with him. On our way to the course I repeatedly thought, *Your goal is bonding with your dad. This is what matters. It doesn't matter how you play, you're here to have fun.*

We didn't go to the driving range. We went straight to the first hole and I teed up a ball, took a couple practice swings, then took a real swing. I made amazing contact, it easily went over 300 yards. There was one slight problem - it could not be any further out of bounds. I'm almost certain I broke someone's window to their house or car.

A few years ago I would have thrown my driver in the fairway in disgust, but now I had a smile like the Grinch after he returned all the gifts back to Whoville. *See? You hit it out of bounds, but you still are having fun. You can only improve from here,* I thought.

Become the Ace

I set up ball number two and took another swing. I hit it even farther this time, *but* it was still out of bounds by a mile. Again, I had a smile on my face. I thought, *how can I be doing this poorly and still be having fun?* My brain immediately answered, *It's a beautiful day and I'm here with my dad.*

I hit four more golf balls and was crushing all of them, but all were nowhere near being in play. After each swing, I was having more and more fun. I was getting tired from swinging so much and let my dad take his swing.

While I was standing there I thought about the question he asked me about years ago, "Do you want to be good *or* do you want to have fun?" Then I asked myself how I could be good *and* have fun.

I immediately got an answer...follow through! I was making great contact, but because I wasn't following through on my swing I was pushing all my shots to the right.

My dad commented, "It's great that you're having fun, but we are running out of golf balls. How about you just drop a ball in the fairway next to mine and

Become the Ace

play from there?" I replied, "Just one more. I believe I figured it out."

As I was lining up I was thinking, *you don't have to make a choice. You can be good **and** have fun. Just follow through. Just follow through.*

When the driver head made contact with the tee, sparks literally flew and ball number seven went farther than the previous six. Ball number seven was different. Ball number seven was flying straight down the middle of the fairway and as I watched it soar there was no doubt about this shot. I followed through.

"Wow! That was incredible!," my dad exclaimed. "I just needed to follow through. Did you see the spark!?", I asked him. "I sure did," he replied.

My next shot in the fairway was also good, because I followed through. My ball landed ten feet from the hole. I sunk that ten foot putt and ended up with a fifteen on that hole, which eleven over par for the hole.

The score was horrendous, but the insight I gained on that hole was life changing. As we were

Become the Ace

approaching the second hole I started to think about replacing the word "or" with the word "and." It was possible.

I thought about all the questions you ask yourself:

Career *or* family?

Pursue your dream *or* do what pays the bills?

Be an achiever or be happy?

Be serious *or* have fun?

The word "or" puts limitations on you and causes you to have a scarcity mindset. The word "and" removes those limitations and allows you to have an abundance mindset.

You can have more "and" and less "or" in your life, but it will take more planning, effort, and persistence. You really can have it all, but need to start thinking and dreaming bigger. *But,* most importantly, you need to follow through!

Ask for everything you want in life and you'll get the answers you need to make it possible. The answers will create the plan, but if you don't

Become the Ace

practice persistence and you quit before you complete your "swing," you'll go way out of bounds and pay the price for all the windows you break.

The word "and" is the word that gets you there. Commit to following through and you'll have everything you want in life.

Lack of persistence is why many dreams go unlived. Lack of persistence is why so many Aces live their lives as 2s, 3s, and 4s. I know from personal experience how easy it can be. Think about your journey differently.

I made up my mind about two years ago that I wanted to be a professional speaker and writer. I had my heart set on speaking at my graduation, which would have a few hundred people in attendance. I spent days writing and rehearsing.

I asked the school if I could speak and I was told they didn't have time for me. I was crushed. I remember thinking, *How am I ever going to make a career out of this if my own school rejects me?*

Become the Ace

I moped around for a couple days contemplating not even trying to pursue my dream. Then something happened that would change my life and can change yours. I picked up a deck of cards and thought of this analogy: pursuing your dream is like the card game War. Although speaking at my graduation was a big deal, compared to what I want to do with my life, the event was like a six in the card game War.

I was getting bummed out because I wasn't good enough for my school to see me as at least a six or higher. If your dream is to be an Ace this could be a problem.

I imagine this has happened to you too. You are passionate about something and decide to go for it. Then you meet immediate rejection and failure with an obstacle that seems small compared to what you would like to do in the future. Maybe you think, *If I can't get past this, there is no point of even trying.*

Imagine if Michael Jordan, one of the greatest basketball players in history, thought this way. When he was sophomore in high school his didn't make the varsity basketball team. He was 5'10 at the

Become the Ace

time and couldn't dunk(7). Don't give up! You may have just gone through the equivalent of missing a high school varsity basketball team and want to play in the NBA, but you very well be the Michael Jordan of your chosen profession. Again, don't give up!

I know that some have advantages that you don't, whether it be talent, looks, money, etc. However, these aren't usually the obstacles that stop your dream from becoming a reality. It lies in developing the qualities I discuss in this book, and persistence is one of the most important.

Just because you're a 2 now and aren't winning the small battles doesn't mean you can't develop yourself and become an Ace in the future. I've been met with failure and rejection several dozen times this year, but I'm learning persistence.

If you can't handle rejection and failure then you *cannot* succeed at the level you're capable of. Most couldn't handle the rejection that some people have experienced to make their dream come true. The founder of Starbucks, Howard Schultz, is an

Become the Ace

example. He had been turned down for a bank loan 242 times!

That's not a typo. It was 242 times. That is an ultimate form of persistence. That's the challenging thing with pursuing your dream. You may have a strong belief in yourself and your ideas and believe you're an ace, but people have to rely on what they see on the outside.

That's why you may spend your life building up your resume so others can see what you have to offer. It's silly to think the world would operate any other way. For example, maybe you have enough talent to play quarterback in the NFL, but if you've never played college or even high school football it would be crazy to think an NFL team would give you a chance.

You don't go from a 2 to an Ace. You become an Ace my moving up by one or two card values at a time. If it appears you're a 2 to the majority of the world, focus on winning a battle that's valued at a 3. Become a 3 and seek to win a battle that's a 4 and so on.

Become the Ace

Life is much more exciting and your dreams seem much more realistic when you chunk up your dream into several dozen battles instead of one big war. Doing it this way will keep you going when you want to give up and make you happier in the moment.

Sometimes you are good enough in the present moment, but need to find one person to take a chance on you. Sometimes your gift is difficult to put on paper. Persistence can be less difficult if you realize in your heart you're an ace and have something special to offer the world.

When you have that, you can can get a "no" 242 times and still believe 243 will be a "yes."

Some people believe that you should always look forward when pursuing a goal. I don't agree. It's great to look back and see how far you've come. This can give you the confidence to handle the bigger challenges that lie ahead and help you persist.

I've quit several things throughout my life and I wanted to point out one of these scenarios from when I was thirteen. I *hated* reading most of my life.

Become the Ace

But, I decided to give *Harry Potter* a shot and *loved* it. These books were massive compared to the picture books I usually read. I even read the first three books and was eager to start reading the fourth one, *The Goblet of Fire*.

This all changed once I saw the size of the book. It seemed twice as big as the first three *Harry Potter* books. I thought, *there's no way I can read that. It's too much work. I'm just going to have to wait a couple years and hope they make it into a movie.*

I never read the book and waited for the movie. However, it occurred to me that if I looked to see all that I already read I would have seen that the first three books combined had significantly more pages than the fourth. I was at a bookstore and held the first three books in one hand and the fourth book in the other.

If I realized how much reading I had *already* done, I could have kept on reading and read all of the books. It's important to learn from mistakes and it's even better if it can be applied to something larger.

As you develop and work towards your potential, your challenges *should* become larger. That's why

Become the Ace

it's important to look back at every challenge you've overcome and celebrate the times you did things you didn't think you could do. Doing this can prevent you from giving up when the obstacle seems daunting.

Let this Harry Potter example apply to your life. There is one big difference though. If *you* give up on your goals, *no one* is going to do the work for you. You won't be able to watch a movie of your successful life years down the road.

If you are ever going to do something memorable with your life you *must* persist, you *must* keep moving forward. But remember, whenever you are doubting yourself, look back at how far you've come and celebrate it. It will develop the persistence you need to be an Ace

Chapter 10

Communication

"Communication - the human connection - is the
key to personal and career success."

—Paul J. Meyer

If you're shy and introverted, don't panic! You
don't have to be the life of the party to be an
effective communicator.

Become the Ace

The first thing you think of when you hear the word communication is likely how you communicate with others. I will be talking about this, but first let's focus on the communication you have with yourself.

It doesn't matter how much you achieve, if you can't communicate with yourself in a healthy way you are far from successful.

The best communicators seem to focus on achieving their highest potential while contributing to the world *and* being happy a majority of their lives. Many spend most of their lives delaying happiness waiting to achieve something great. This is silly. You can be happy *while* in pursuit of your dreams. You can be happy *during* your obstacles and challenges.

I know first hand being happy in just about every situation is possible, but it does take work. It takes work because often you are on autopilot and you choose to feel a certain way because that's what a majority of people do.

Traffic is an example I love to use. If you work 8 to 5 in a populated area, you're likely going to

Become the Ace

experience traffic going both ways. I know it would be great if it didn't exist and being in traffic can make you angry and frustrated. It's a normal feeling, but does it make sense to feel this way?

I asked myself that question recently and started to laugh. Would getting angry cause traffic to clear up? Would getting angry cause an opening in the middle of the road like the red sea? No! If you drop your car off to get an oil change or you're waiting to be seated at a restaurant and you're told the wait will be an hour and it takes longer than that, will getting upset speed up the process? No! If anything, unloading your frustration on the situation makes the wait longer.

Life can be much better if you drop your expectations, realize inconveniences will be part of life, and communicate happiness to yourself anyway. You can always go to your "happy place." I'm referring to the movie *Happy Gilmore* starring Adam Sandler when I talk about this. However, it doesn't have to be a separate location in your mind. You can create your happy place by what you're choosing to focus on.

Become the Ace

Using traffic as an example, that time you have to yourself can be valuable. Instead of getting angry, flipping someone off, and punching your steering wheel, you can think about how your day went. You can ask yourself what your learned and what you can do to improve yourself. You can listen to audiobooks that can instruct and inspire to become an ace even faster.

You could also spend that time thinking about all that you have to be grateful for. You could use that time to call family and friends you say you don't have time for. It seems unfair how some people seem to be happy in all situations, but it's not magic. You can be happy too. It all lies in how you communicate with yourself in the situations that are taking place in your life.

You may find this odd, but there is the one man in his 50s who bags groceries and probably makes $10 per hour. I consider him to be a successful person. His smile lights up the room and he always seems to be happy. Whenever I go shopping I hope to see him because his positive energy rubs off me. Every time I see him I think, *That guy is successful.* Maybe

Become the Ace

you think there's no way you'd be considered a success making $10 per hour.

I thought the same thing the first time I said this about him. Look at it this way: there are people who are perfectionists who are multimillionaires and over-achievers in every sense of the word but *cannot* allow themselves to be happy in the moment. The present moment is the moment you live in and if you can't experience happiness right now, then you need to change your communication.

I'm not saying to lose your drive to achieve something incredible in your life. I'm saying allow yourself to be happy *while* you work towards your ideal self. It took me awhile, but after reading and listening about the psychology terms of self-ideal, self-image, and self-esteem repeatedly, I started to grasp these concepts and experience more happiness and joy in my life. If I can do it, I know you can too.

Here's a basic definition for each of these three terms:

Become the Ace

Self-ideal: This is you at your best, where you have your highest values and are living life at your potential. Your self-ideal is you as an Ace.

Self-image: Often referred as the "inner mirror." This is how you see yourself and it is a major factor in how you behave.

Self-esteem: How you feel about yourself.

All three work together and factor into your ability to experience happiness. The main issue I find is that your self-image is often not in line with your self-ideal. That's okay! Whenever these two aren't in line, the most convenient thing to do is to make a clever excuse or to deflect blame on someone else.

This is the easiest way to protect our ego, but over time it lowers your self-esteem and makes it difficult to experience happiness. That's why it's important to address your self-image in an honest way. It's important to look at the inner-mirror without distorting it. Focus on what you like about yourself, but also what you don't like.

Here's something wonderful I've realized: you can change your self-image in an instant and radically

Become the Ace

alter your life. To make permanent, long-lasting changes you cannot simply alter your behavior, you have to change the reflection in your inner-mirror.

Dr Joyce Brothers has stated, "You cannot perform in a manner inconsistent with the way you see yourself."

Simply put, to start getting results faster start seeing yourself as an Ace on the inside. It's okay if you realize you're a two on the outside. You will naturally be drawn to do what's necessary to be consistent with how you see yourself on the inside.

You may not have a clue how you'll become an ace on the outside but that's okay. All the questions you ask about making your dream come true have an answer. Everything falls in line once you start to see yourself at your best on the inside.

It's difficult for many because they often need validation from others to allow themselves to see an ace on the inside. It's possible you want to avoid looking delusional because you feel you have no proof to see yourself in this light. Here's a simple fix: don't tell anyone. You can keep the inner mirror image you have to yourself.

Become the Ace

You won't have to tell anyone anyway because it will be a matter of time before your inner self reflects your outer self. But it's not until you start communicating to yourself that you're Ace that you become one.

Now let's talk about communication with other people. It doesn't matter if you're extroverted or introverted, communication with others is important. If you feel you're quiet and reserved that's okay.

Susan Cain has pointed out introverts have made an amazing impact in the world in her book *Quiet: The Power of Introverts in a World That Can't Stop Talking*. She has also done a TED talk on this subject.

I'm confident you will come up with great ideas throughout your life. Also, if you continue to invest in yourself and strive to reach your potential you'll naturally acquire more responsibility and find yourself in leadership positions.

If communicating and leading others scares you it's okay! Both of these qualities can be developed. They don't happen naturally. They come with practice.

Become the Ace

The best thing to do is try to start having more conversations and make listening your primary focus. You may be surprised when people tell you you're a great conversationalist when you ask questions and seek to listen sincerely to the answers.

Also, when you dream big and have a vision it will involve the help of others. Being able to articulate your plans to others will be crucial to making your vision a reality. Again, the best thing you can do is practice. Improving communication starts with yourself. Once you get this right, you may find it easier to communicate with others.

Chapter 11

Focus

"Realize deeply that the present moment is all you ever have. Make the Now the primary focus of your life."

— Eckhart Tolle

There are times we are unsuccessful making our dreams come true because we don't pay attention. Maybe because what we're doing seems to have nothing to do with developing our skills,

Become the Ace

but it does. I know from personal experience that failing to do this can be painful.

In 7th grade, I decided that I was going to start playing football and be the team's quarterback. I had *all* the skills. I could consistently throw ten touchdowns per game playing as Kurt Warner of the St. Louis Rams on the video game *Madden,* and one time at a carnival I won a stuffed teddy bear by throwing a football through a tire.

I had recently moved from Florida to South Carolina and the team had already been practicing for about a week. The coach knew I was coming that day and asked the captain of the team, Blake, to hang out in the locker room while everyone else was on the field to get me all the equipment I needed.

It was the first time I've ever been in a locker room and the smell was difficult to describe. One person described it as "tangy crotch." I don't know how those two words got put together, but it sounds right.

Become the Ace

Blake gave me a firm handshake and said, "Welcome to the team. What position are you going for?"

"Quarterback," I replied

"That's great. We could use one. Let me give you a piece of advice. Avoid Josh at all costs. He will crush you. I don't even have to give you his football number because you'll know who I'm talking about when you see him."

After taking ten minutes to put on all my equipment, Blake and I met the other players out on the field. They had just finished stretching and everyone was off the field near the equipment that improves your footwork.

It didn't look like I would be throwing a football and felt the drill didn't apply to me. I decided to focus on something more important - what I would be eating once I got home. I had narrowed it down to a massive bowl of lucky charms *or* and ham sandwich loaded with crushed nacho cheese Doritos.

Become the Ace

I was turned completely away from the drill and had given this life or death decision all my focus. I would soon find out that not paying attention to this drill would cause me a lot of pain. My focus went back to the drill once the head coach yelled, "Let's go! Somebody step up!"

I looked around and everyone seemed to be avoiding this drill. I asked one of the guys what we needed to do. He replied, "You just need to hold a football and make sure your feet hit all the boxes." *Simple enough. Why did everyone seem so afraid?*, I thought.

I told the coach, "I'll do it." As I stepped up in front the boxed chains, I realized Blake was right about Josh. *What is an NFL linebacker doing here at a middle school practice? His neck is thicker than my legs.* He was standing ten feet behind where the boxed chain ended.

As much as I was in awe of the size of Josh, I was now focused on my footwork. I needed to hit every box and my eyes were looking down to make sure I would succeed. There was one important detail about this drill that I was not told about. It was that

Become the Ace

once you finished the drill another player would be tackling you.

I found out that the coach explained this during my cereal/sandwich crisis and told us to get low and protect ourselves from the hit. I, unfortunately, did *not* protect myself. As my foot hit the last box I was jogging completely upright wondering who I should hand the football off to.

Within seconds I found myself on the ground thinking all my ribs were broken and wondering if I'd ever get up. There's no doubt about it. Josh put a highlight worthy tackle on me. The entire team pronounced in unison, "Ohhhh!" The movie *Friday* starring Chris Tucker and Ice Cube was popular at the time and one kid acted out one of the memorable scenes when Ice Cube's character, Craig, knocked out the neighborhood's tormentor, Deebo.

As I was laying on the ground, one kid stood right near me and shouted, "You just got knocked the hell out!." I couldn't argue with him. It was a vicious hit. After that drill, becoming a quarterback became less appealing.

Become the Ace

Deep down I knew football wasn't for me. The rest of the practice I did my best to be an observer and I kept my helmet on so the other guys wouldn't see my crying. When practice was over my mom and sister were in the parking lot to pick me up. My sister asked, "Have you been crying?"

In immediate defense I exclaimed, "No! I've been working really hard and it's hot. It's sweat. I haven't been crying." It turns out that I didn't break any ribs, but I had some severe bruising that would take a couple weeks to go away.

I realized how fortunate I am that this happened to me. I'll list all the takeaways now:

#1 Being good at Madden and throwing a football through a tire at a carnival does *not* qualify you to be a quarterback in real life.

#2 Often we fail to realize how important the present moment is. There is always something you can be doing that could develop your skills even though it doesn't seem like it. For example, a quarterback needs great footwork and needs to be able to protect himself when being tackled.

Become the Ace

It reminded me of the original *Karate Kid* starring Ralph Macchio. His character wanted to start learning the moves of karate and was frustrated when he was told to paint a house and "wax on, wax off." He thought these activities were pointless.

Often developing your skills involves boring tasks like these. However, these are fundamentals. It's easy to do the fun stuff, but when you're serious about developing your craft, you realize how important fundamentals are.

#3 Stay mindful. I may have been hungry, but if I was present in the moment and focused on that drill, I probably would have avoided going first. At the very least, I would have been able to lower my shoulders and absorb some of that thundering hit Josh laid on me. Planning for your future is important, but moments like that drill, was not the time for me.

It takes discipline to focus on living in the moment, observing everything around you and making the best use of your time. It's worth it though. It dramatically decreases your chances of getting hit by the Joshes of life.

Chapter 12

---◦◦◦---

Balance

"The hardest thing to find in life is balance."

—Celine Dion

The quote seems random, but what she said ties in perfectly here.

This topic came to me when I was eating Lucky Charms. I've generally had a "work first then play later" attitude towards everything in life. With this

Become the Ace

mentality it was natural for me to eat the "wood parts" (the parts that aren't marshmallows) first and have nothing but marshmallows to enjoy at the end.

The problem is that eating *only* the marshmallow part was too sweet. It wasn't satisfying. Maybe the makers of this cereal, General Mills, know what they're doing. There is a reason the "wood parts" exist. Maybe life is just like the cereal Lucky Charms; there's a balance you may spend your whole life trying to find, but the prize is worth it. The prize is true happiness.

Finding the right balance in life is will always be a work in progress. As much as I don't want this to be true, it's not all or nothing and too much of anything can be toxic.

During my first toxicology class in graduate school, the professor opened her talk by sharing a quote from Paracelsus, a 16th century scientist referred to by some as the father of toxicology. He wrote, "the dose makes the poison." My professor explained *everything* in life is toxic, it's all a matter of how much you consume.

Become the Ace

She explained drinking too much water could cause water intoxication and too many vegetables could cause minerals to build up in your body and cause kidney stones. I've learned to question what I hear and I recommend you do this same.

Everything in life can be toxic, she said. I'll share with you now some aspects of life I've tested.

#1 Can you be too nice?

There are different types of being nice. One can be when you're driven to be liked. Maybe growing up you'd give someone a toy or loan them money in exchange for them becoming your friend. In these scenarios you're being nice for the sole purpose of being accepted.

Several men have this when it comes to dating: it has been called "nice guy syndrome." You feel like you have to drop everything you're doing and do whatever the woman needs. You may even spend money buying expensive dinners and gifts you can't afford to prove your worth.

If this is describes you, then this is toxic. The strange thing is that if you put people up on a pedestal and worship them, then you lose connection. People want to be treated normally and being *too* nice can make them feel uncomfortable and cause them to lose respect for you.

Another thing is some people will take advantage of you. You can be working so hard to gain approval from someone to feel better about yourself, but in some cases it can do the complete opposite if you take it too far.

Another part of being too nice doesn't involve approval seeking. Maybe you want nothing from this person. You just want to help them have the life you have. They ask for money and you can give it to them. They ask for your help and you give it to them. It can make you feel good helping someone in need.

I think we all at times need someone to give us a "fish" to eat. However, once we've been "fed" it's our responsibility to teach them how to fish. Sometimes you have to say no, and let people take responsibility for their lives. It can difficult, because you love and care about this person, but if you

Become the Ace

never force them to fish for themselves, learned helplessness occurs.

Learned helplessness occurs when an animal is repeatedly subjected to an aversive stimulus that it cannot escape. Eventually, the animal will stop trying to avoid the stimulus and behave as if it is utterly helpless to change the situation. Even when opportunities to escape are presented, this learned helplessness will prevent any action.(8)

For example, you can have somebody that doubts themselves constantly. They may say the person they like is out of their league, they could never land the job they want, or they ask you if they look fat. In the beginning providing encouragement and support is the right thing to do. However, at a certain point, it's toxic. The person may rely so heavily on your assurance that they will never develop the self-confidence they need to become an Ace.

It may not be in a malicious way, but they are using you. The greatest way to break this is to start playing the song "Use Me" by Bill Withers whenever you think about them. This little trick can

Become the Ace

help you get over being nice at the point it's toxic for yourself and others.

At a certain point your responses to the following comments should change. "He or she is way too good for me." "I'll never get the promotion." "I'm so fat and ugly." Now it's time for you to say, "You're right." This can really throw them off, especially if you've become their go-to person for encouragement and support.

But being too nice is toxic. Ralph Waldo Emerson has stated, "We become what we think about all day long." If anyone is going to become an Ace in life, they have to believe it for *themselves*. In the early stages it's okay to have others plant positive seeds in your mind, but eventually it will be time for you to start planting the seeds on your own.

#2 Can you be too optimistic?

I asked this question after somebody gave something interesting to think about. I said, "I'm optimistic no matter what. You can never be too positive." This person replied, "Okay. You should pick up the next hitchhiker holding a machete you find because you're optimistic he won't chop your

Become the Ace

head off." I realized taking some caution once in awhile may be a good idea.

It's possible you spend your whole life being negative and thinking about what could go wrong. But then you decide it's draining your energy and decide that positivity is the way to go. Once you switch to a positive mindset you feel you never want to be negative again.

Recently, I approached my goals as failure not being an option. If I came up with a backup plan then that would mean I didn't believe in myself. I now know this is ridiculous. It's foolish not to have backup plans. In fact, thinking about the worst case scenario often reduces stress and gives you even more confidence to pursue your goals.

For example, think about applying to get into a college or a job you want. You can ask, *what will happen if I don't get it?* Your response should be: *it will be a great learning experience and I'll find out what I'll need to do to get it the next school year or the next time a job like this opens up.*

Is it possible you make situations in life more stressful than they need to be? If you don't succeed

Become the Ace

it's *not* the end of the world and it *won't* kill you. Also having the belief that things happen for a reason also helps you get over rejection. From personal experience, once I've come up with the worst case scenario and have accepted it, my stress is almost completely eliminated.

You can apply for the job, ask out that person, or set that goal that seems to have a low chance of success. The amazing thing is, with the pressure taken off of you, you may be surprised when you succeed because of the confidence you're projecting.

When you're optimistic you generally don't have many problems. Instead they're challenges or opportunities. However, there are things in your life that are out of your control and they will bother you. Ignoring them and telling yourself you're ungrateful for complaining about them is toxic.

Practicing gratitude and focusing on solutions to your problems wipes out ninety-five percent of your issues. However, it's okay to vent about the other five percent to the people closest to you. Talking to random strangers is not the way to go.

Become the Ace

The best thing is to share your frustrations with the select view who love and support you.

As long as you're there for them and let them vent to you about the problems they can't seem to get over, you should feel comfortable doing the same. As someone pointed out to me recently, "life can't be lollipops and rainbows all the time." Being optimistic *nearly* one hundred percent of the time and not *all* the time seems to be the way to go.

#3 Can you want your dream too much?

I've come to realize that living the dream has less to do with winning a certain award or getting asked for your autograph, and more to do with the feeling you get from going after what you want. It doesn't matter what you achieve; if you're not happy a majority of the time you're not an Ace.

Also, if you don't have people in your life to share your success with, you're not an ace. Putting too much of yourself into your professional development can be toxic. There is nothing impressive about excelling at one area in your life if that means you are mediocre in other areas. This lack of balance in life is toxic.

Become the Ace

Think about Ebenezer Scrooge from Charles Dickens', *A Christmas Carol.* He was an exceptional businessman, but didn't have balance and was a "humbug." It's not just about success; it's also about being happy.

You've heard the saying "a jack of all trades is a master of none." This doesn't always apply to life. True happiness comes from living in abundance and developing in *all* areas of your life. Denis Waitley's book, *Seeds of Greatness* can help you realize the importance of balanced living.

There are eight areas of life that the author has you take a self assessment on. It can be a eye-opener for you. You may feel you're successful, but it's possible life can be even more enjoyable with more balance.

Reading personal development books has a way of making you more disciplined. Many books talk about the Pareto Principle, also known as the 80/20 rule, and encourage you to do the highest priority tasks most of the time to increase productivity.

When you constantly ask yourself, *what is the most important thing I can do right now?* you find an

Become the Ace

answer. However, sometimes your answer isn't always right. Maybe it *would* be highly productive to practice on your craft, study, or promote your products to potential customers. But doing this too much can be toxic.

Sometimes it's best to take your mind off your work and spend the rest of the afternoon with your family, volunteer to help someone in need, or spend a few hours watching a football game. It's natural to have areas of your life in which you excel more than others, but the life of the Ace involves constant development in all areas.

Too much of *anything* is toxic. It is incredibly easy to focus so much on your ultimate destination that you forget to have fun on the journey. Life is about developing your juggling skills. I've asked a few people and I've been told juggling one or two things exceptionally well doesn't count as juggling.

The true Aces know how to juggle *all* the components of life. Sometimes you'll have to make sacrifices to practice balanced living. It's possible to live the life of an Ace and not have your passion be your career.

Become the Ace

I've changed my view on this after reading *Big Magic* by Elizabeth Gilbert. Sometimes your job may not be your passion and your passion takes a back seat to develop all the other areas of your life.

However, passion must be present. She stated in the book, "If your job is a sacrifice, do your passion on the side." Balance is key to living the life of an Ace. It takes a lot of skill and discipline, but the ultimate prize - true happiness - is worth the price.

Chapter 13

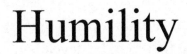

Humility

"Humility is the solid foundation of all virtues"

—Confucius

Look at humility as being able to harness the power that comes from admitting you don't know. It seems that those that believe they "know it all" are the ones who know the least. It does take courage admitting you don't know something, but you don't have to know everything. There are

Become the Ace

billions of people on this earth and people will always know things you don't, and vice versa.

Wouldn't it be better to share our knowledge and use it to make the world a better place? Plus, admitting your limitations and the knowledge you're lacking is one of the fastest ways to becoming successful. This is because you can overcome your limitations through development. If it's something that can't be developed, then you can team up with someone who is strong where you're weak.

Everything is possible in life. You just need to know how. The amazing thing is that many people have found the answers to the questions you're asking. Many have even wrote them down in books.

It can be frustrating spending your whole life trying to figure things out on your own, when the answers to your problem were discovered by someone a hundred years ago. Why is it so hard for us to have others with more wisdom and guidance help us?

Maybe because your pride is at stake. It's also possible many look at asking for help as an indication of weakness and admitting they don't

Become the Ace

know something as a sign of incompetence. We don't want people to think we're fools. You're going to look like a fool from time to time.

For example, I once put foil in the microwave. I repeat, *I once put foil in the microwave*! Did I feel like a fool when everyone around me asked, "How do you not know this?" Yes. In their defense I was in my twenties and probably should have known this. Yet, I laugh about it now. Plus, I learned my lesson and have never put foil in the microwave again!

When I was younger I had this issue in school too. Teachers would ask often, after explaining a topic, "Does anyone have any questions?" Oftentimes I had questions, but didn't want to appear stupid in front of everyone. Fortunately, there always seemed to be a group of people that would ask the teacher to explain it again. With these other people I was able to get my questions answered without looking like a fool.

Recently, I changed my way of thinking after I asked this question: "Is it better that others *think* I'm a fool for asking something *or* is it better to *be* a fool

Become the Ace

for having the opportunity to get my question answered and passing it up?"

Maybe it takes time to mature and focus on what's important. Near the last year of college I realized how ridiculous it was waiting for other people to step up and ask for clarification. One day, a concept wasn't clear to me, but as usual the teacher asked, "Any questions?" I was nervous, but asked if the teacher could explain it again.

Something great happened. I was now okay admitting I didn't know things. Also, the person sitting beside me tapped my shoulder and thanked me for asking the teacher to explain it again. He was confused, too. That's when I realized that when something doesn't make sense to you, odds are you aren't the only one. Plus, people usually don't criticize you; often they thank you for being brave and doing something they were afraid to do.

Every successful person has gotten help along the way. Find a way to let mentors help you and read books that direct you to where you'd like to go. Doing this will help you become an Ace, and faster than you ever imagined.

Become the Ace

There is psychology behind our struggle to admit we don't know. It's called the "Endowment Effect." Nineteen-seventies economist Richard Thaler coined the term the "Endowment Effect," and it explained your irrational tendency to overvalue something just because you own it (9).

Thaler evaluated two scenarios. The first scenario involves a man who owns a case of good wine he bought in the late 1950s for $5 a bottle. When a wine merchant offers to buy his wine for $100 a bottle the man refuses, even though he never paid more than $35 for a bottle of wine in his life. The second scenario involves a man who mows his own lawn and receives an offer from his neighbor's son to mow his lawn for $8. The man refuses, even though he wouldn't mow his neighbor's same-sized lawn for less than $20.

Thaler put it: "Goods included in the individual's endowment will be more highly valued than those not held in the endowment, *ceteris paribus*." This makes sense. Ever have somebody try to buy something from you at or above market value but you refuse to part with it? Maybe it had too much sentimental value. Whatever the case, you valued it

Become the Ace

higher that it was likely worth. Many believe this occurs because humans generally are more afraid of losing something instead of gaining something pleasurable.

The endowment effect applies to material possessions, but then it occurred to me that it's possible it happens with our thoughts, too. The thoughts we hold shape our identity. As long as you believe you're weak for asking for help, stupid for admitting something you don't know, or a fool for admitting you made a mistake, you will likely refuse to make adjustments that will improve your life out of fear of losing the identity of who you think you are.

It's possible your beliefs don't match up with your actions anyway. Try looking at it in a different way if you're struggling to ask for help. Your parents helped you by bringing you into this world, you get help from a doctor when you're sick, you get help from an accountant when you do your taxes, you get help from the makers of your car whenever you drive. You already are dependent on help from so many people. Why not allow yourself to receive help to live out your life's purpose?

Become the Ace

The best way to get over this is to start possessing the idea of humility and looking at yourself as a never-ending work in progress. You should stop possessing the idea of pride and looking at yourself as a finished product in the present moment. Humility will help you grow while pride will help you shrink.

Humility is a quality that is universally admired. Those who are humble separate what they accomplish from who they are. Because of this, their ego never gets in the way of taking advice or asking for help.

It's a struggle to separate the two, but remember you're an ace on the inside no matter what. The only way to become an Ace on the inside and out is to practice humility. The only way to become an ace on the inside and out is to find the courage to say "I don't know."

When you're humble you allow yourself to take all feedback in and analyze it, use it to make yourself better, *and* do it while keeping a smile on your face. It seems humility is a quality all the Aces of the world are taking advantage of.

Become the Ace

Without question, admitting you don't know helps you reach your potential. However, there is another benefit. It involves other people. It's natural for us to generalize. If someone cuts you off in traffic or yells at you for no reason you tend to link the behavior with their identity and not evaluate the behavior as separate from who they are.

For example, when someone cuts you off in traffic, you generally say, "she's a jerk" or if someone at works snaps at you you say, "he's an angry person." But it's not fair to label someone from one event.

It's better for your mental health to give others the benefit of the doubt and then seek to understand what is causing this behavior. But it's better to take a step further and admit you don't know.

Imagine someone you cared about approached you for help. They are trying to tell you they're depressed and thinking about ending their life, but you won't let them talk. All you do is tell them how selfish and inconsiderate they are for never helping you when you need them.

Become the Ace

After several minutes of attacking their character without having all the facts you listen to what they have to say. Odds are you'll say, "I'm so sorry for what I said. *I didn't know* you were struggling with that."

It's a dark example, but things like this are more common that you think. Many are too quick to make snap judgements on others when oftentimes the other person has a reason for behaving the way they do. I've been guilty of this several times throughout my life.

From experience, I've found that giving people the benefit of the doubt and admitting that you don't know what the person is going through can help you forgive quickly and not let it affect your personal happiness.

Telling someone, "I don't know, but I'd like to understand and help you in any way I can," increases the person's chances of opening up to you and allowing you to make a positive difference in their life.

The humility that comes from "I don't know" allows you to use all the resources available to you

Become the Ace

to facilitate your growth and development, but also allows you to practice compassion and forgiveness.

To sum up the topic of humility and using this quality to develop as an ace and live the good life, I'll reference a TED talk. It is from Tai Lopez's, _Why I read a book a day (and why you should too): The law of 33%_, "Everybody wants the good life, but not everybody is willing to be humble. You must be humble."

Chapter 14

---○---

Final Thoughts

Thinking about what you've read in this book, and any book for that matter, and deciding what ideas you want to accept or reject is crucial. I've been amazed how many times there are conflicting views on what it takes to be successful. The best thing to do is keep an open mind, listen to both sides, and then decide what *you* believe.

After reading several dozen personal development books this past year I've realized the keys to becoming an ace are already known and people have used them before you were born.

Become the Ace

However, there is a *big* difference from knowing something and emotionally internalizing it so that it changes your actions and leads to long-lasting change.

For example, you may know that mindfulness is important, but providing you with a story about a tackle that almost put me in the hospital may stick with you longer than someone just telling you that "mindfulness is important."

Tony Robbins stated, "Eighty percent of success is psychology and twenty percent of success is mechanics." The biggest portion of success involves acquiring the proper mindset and my goal is to make acquiring the proper mindset as simple as possible.

I don't want to discount the mechanics because they're crucial. If you want to be surgeon, it doesn't matter how incredible your mindset is, you'll need to go to medical school. However, by applying what you learn in personal development books, you can take the necessary steps to becoming an Ace

I know there's nothing earth shattering in the book, but I'm certain you've come across topics that were

Become the Ace

presented in a different way. That has been my goal so for in my books: Read complex material and break it down to make it as simple as possible. Then develop a mindset that allows you overcome all of life's challenges with a smile on your face.

This is why I spent most of my life thinking on how to present known material in a different way. If you've read several books and it still hasn't "clicked" for you yet, keep searching. All it takes is one story or idea that resonates with you and changes your way of thinking and leads to you becoming an Ace in life.

Motivation isn't something you acquire once and you're set for life. Finding motivation is a daily practice. Zig Ziglar stated, "People often say that motivation doesn't last. Well, neither does bathing - that's why we recommend it daily."

I'd recommend reading or listening to personal development topics on a daily basis for at least thirty minutes. My concern is that you'll hear something motivating, but it wears off in a couple days because the challenges of life got in the way.

Become the Ace

There are so many amazing people who share their wisdom. Don't get it all from one person. I wouldn't expect you to agree with everything you read in this book. No one is one hundred percent on the same page with another person. That's a great thing. We all have the ability to think in different ways.

There is so much benefit to listening to people present material at different angles. You may connect with one author more than the other, but everyone is capable of providing a nugget of wisdom that causes you change how you live your life.

I truly believe *everyone* has a gift to offer this world. I truly believe everyone *can* become an Ace in life. Your journey starts *now*. If you can get in the habit of practicing all the topics discussed in this book and develop a never-ending drive to develop yourself, you're already an Ace!

There's plenty of success to go around. I'm rooting for you! I hope some idea or story jumped out at you and caused you to think, *I've found most of my life that things went in one ear and out the other, but*

Become the Ace

when it was presented in a different way, things started to sink in.

Finding new ways to present material has becoming an obsession of mine. I want to do whatever it takes for you to see what I see when I look at you, an **Ace** that can do anything you set your mind to. An **Ace** the world needs and will never forget. An **Ace** that inspires others to be more, do more, and live more.

I know you're going to do something special with your life. I know I'll be able to tell your story of success soon! Since I don't know your name so I'll call you Ace instead!

We'll talk soon.

Your friend,
Michael

Contact Information

I f there is anything in this book that helped you, or if you have questions for me, I'd love to hear from you!

If you are interested in having me speak about topics discussed in this book, you can reach me at my website: michaelunks.com

Email: unksmichael@gmail.com

Facebook: Michael Unks

Twitter: @MichaelUnks

Thanks again for reading my book, and I hope you will start living the life you've always wanted!

-Michael

Acknowledgements

God: You will always be the first on my list. Once I accepted you in my heart I found my peace, passion, and purpose. I love my life and I'm incredibly blessed because of you. I wake up every morning grateful you've given me another day on this Earth and ask that you continue guide me to where you want me to serve.

All the men and women that are serving, or who have served, our country: You are the true heroes who often go unnoticed. It's your tremendous courage and sacrifice that allows many of us to pursue our dreams. Please know that what you do doesn't go unnoticed by me, and I'll be forever grateful to all of you.

147

Become the Ace

Ruth Unks: Thanks for editing my book. You've helped me make this book a lot better.

Kayleigh Lot: Thank you for proofreading my book. You're the best!

Kurt Olson: Thanks for all your guidance and encouragement. You're a great friend!

Tiki Vietri: Thank you for all the hours we've spent bouncing ideas off each other. You've helped me tremendously!

Ida Svenningson: Thank you for designing my cover. Your work is incredible!

Thatlevel.com: Thank you guys for making my incredible website.

Happy Self-Publishing: Thank you all for formatting my book for Kindle and for paperback.

To anyone else I didn't mention please know that you're appreciated! The feedback and encouragement I've received from many people has made it easier for me to keep pursuing my dream of helping people become Aces!

Resources

1. Rosenthal, R.; Jacobson, L. (1968). *Pygmalion in the Classroom*. New York: Holt, Rinehart & Winston.

2. http://www.psych2go.net/pratfall-effect-imperfect-makes-likeable/

3. Aronson, E., Willerman, B., & Floyd, J. (1966). The effect of a pratfall on increasing interpersonal attractiveness. Psychonomic Science.

4 http://deadspin.com/5908196/we-talkin-bout-practice-allen-iversons-famous-rant-was-10-years-ago-today

5.http://www.alleydog.com/glossary/definition.php?term=Spotlight%20Effect

6. http://pediapedia.org/library/do-more-faster/trust-me-your-idea-is-worthless-tim-ferriss

Become the Ace

7. http://www.newsweek.com/missing-cut-382954

8. http://psychology.about.com/od/lindex/f/earned-helplessness.htm

9. http://bigthink.com/insights-of-genius/rethinking-the-endowment-effect-how-ownership-effects-our-valuations

10. http://www.scientificamerican.com/article/learning-by-surprise/ (novelty promotes memory)

11. http://www.lifehack.org/articles/featured/the-science-of-setting-goals.html

12. http://www.entrepreneur.com/article/225356

13. http://www.cnn.com/2014/03/25/health/brain-crafting-benefits/ (Hobbies and effect on dopamine)

14. http://bebrainfit.com/increase-dopamine/

15. http://www.uptodate.com/contents/cocaine-use-disorder-in-adults-epidemiology-pharmacology-clinical-manifestations-medical-consequences-and-diagnosis/abstract/29

16 *The Art of Work* by Jeff Goins

17 *The Entrepreneur Roller* Coaster by Darren Hardy

Become the Ace

18 http://impossiblehq.com/parkinsons-law/

19 Simon HA, Chase WG. Skill in chess. *Am Sci.* 1973;
61:394–403.

20 Ericsson, K. A. (2008). Deliberate practice and
acquisition of expert performance: A general overview.
Academic Emergency Medicine.15(11), 988-994

21. Mitchell, Terence R.; Daniels, Denise (2003).
"Motivation". In Walter C. Borman, Daniel R. Ilgen,
Richard J. Klimoski. *Handbook of Psychology (volume 12).*
John Wiley & Sons, Inc. p. 229. ISBN 0-471-38408-9.

22 https://en.wikipedia.org/wiki/Pygmalion_effect

23. http://study.com/academy/lesson/self-fulfilling-
prophecies-in-psychology-definition-examples.html

Printed in Great Britain
by Amazon